IN SICKNESS AND IN HEALTH

IN SICKNESS AND IN HEALTH

LOVE, DISABILITY, AND A QUEST TO UNDERSTAND THE PERILS AND PLEASURES OF INTERABLED ROMANCE

—◆—

BEN MATTLIN

BEACON PRESS
BOSTON

BEACON PRESS
Boston, Massachusetts
www.beacon.org

Beacon Press books
are published under the auspices of
the Unitarian Universalist Association of Congregations.

21 20 19 18   8 7 6 5 4 3 2 1

This book is printed on acid-free paper that meets the uncoated paper
ANSI/NISO specifications for permanence as revised in 1992.

Text design and composition by Kim Arney

Portions of this manuscript previously appeared, in very different form,
in *New Mobility* magazine and the *New York Times*.

Library of Congress Cataloging-in-Publication Data

Names: Mattlin, Ben, author.
Title: In sickness and in health : love, disability, and a quest to
understand the perils and pleasures of interabled romance / Ben Mattlin.
Description: Boston : Beacon Press, 2017.
Identifiers: LCCN 2017004699 (print) | LCCN 2017021209 (e-book) |
ISBN 9780807058558 (e-book) | ISBN 9780807058541 (hardcover : alk. paper)
Subjects: LCSH: People with disabilities—United States—Case studies. |
Couples—United States—Case studies. | Interpersonal relations—United
States—Case studies.
Classification: LCC HV1553 (e-book) | LCC HV1553 .M3727 2017 (print) |
DDC 306.8087/0973—dc23
LC record available at https://lccn.loc.gov/2017004699

For my wife and daughters:
I love you. Maybe that's all that needs to be said.

———◆———

Three years on, I was still the one washing his body every other day with a wet cloth, shaving his face, clipping his nails, cutting his hair. I fed him his food and helped him on the bedpan, and I wiped him clean, the way you do an infant, and I washed the soiled diapers I pinned on him. In that time, we had developed between us an unspoken language born of familiarity and routine, and, inevitably, a degree of previously unthinkable informality had seeped into our relationship.

—KHALED HOSSEINI, *And the Mountains Echoed*

For most of us, there's nothing wrong that couldn't be fixed with civil rights and some really gnarly sex!

—PAUL K. LONGMORE, in conversation

CONTENTS

INTRODUCTION

BACK IN 2012, I had the good fortune of publishing a book. *That* book. You know, the one able-bodied people are always telling crips to do because they're sure it would be "so inspirational!"— in short, a memoir about growing up with a severe disability and somehow prospering.

Indeed, being unable to walk or even scratch my nose hadn't prevented me from going to Harvard. I was one of the first quadriplegics to matriculate, if not *the* first (bragging rights not yet fully established). It hadn't prevented me from marrying (and *staying* married for twenty-six years now, and counting), having two delightful children, and forging a career as a freelance journalist. But of course, you already know all that, if you've read my first book.

Miracle Boy Grows Up introduced people to spinal muscular atrophy, the neuromuscular incapacity with which I was born. I have no muscles but full sensation (more about that later). I learned to live with it just as the world was learning to live with people with disabilities as a political force, a civil rights movement. But what to do for a follow-up? I'm not Mary Karr! My life only has one book in it.

Some readers were insistent. A number of them suggested I delve deeper into my marriage, expose the secret spats and salacious highlights. But I didn't want to turn myself and my wife, Mary Lois (who does not have a disability of her own, poor thing), into gossip fodder, thank you very much.

Yet the nugget of an idea began to form.

✦ ✦ ✦

Surely, we can't be the only "interabled" couple, for lack of a better term. Quick research showed that, although the statistics are unreliable, there are many marriages between people with and people without disabilities. And as the population ages and medical and technological advances enable people to survive illnesses and injuries in greater numbers than ever before, more and more folks are finding themselves in more or less our situation.

To the media and general public, though, this kind of amatory partnering is often treated as an odd phenomenon. Not long ago, the cover of *People* magazine flaunted the marriage of Gabby Giffords—the brain-injured former congresswoman—and her husband, astronaut Mark Kelly, as a "special but unconventional love affair." Is that supposed to be flattering? This treacly hooey could give you diabetes!

I also keep hearing and reading about the aging population, this wave of debility and decay that's creating a "caregiving crisis" (*New York Times*, February 26, 2014, among others). To me, this trend dovetails with the worrisome news of veterans who are returning from Iraq and Afghanistan with disabling injuries—the wounded warriors with young spouses who don't know how to cope with their disabilities.

I know strangers frequently regard M.L. and me as either tragic or noble. (We're neither.) At the root of all this wonder and puzzlement, I think, is simple curiosity: *How do they get by? Will they be all right?* To put it another way, what people really ponder is: *What kinds of pressures does disability put on a marriage?* (The former activist in me protests: These quandaries are predicated on outmoded, unflattering presumptions that people with disabilities are nothing but burdens and liabilities! Certainly we bring more to our marriages than our bodily limitations!)

In an age when interracial and interfaith marriages are common, it seems odd that romances like ours still leave people perplexed and awestruck. Many times I've heard M.L. calmly explain to the inquisitive, "I simply fell in love with a guy who happened to be in a wheelchair. Nothing noble or self-sacrificing about it." (In funny moments, she's added, "It's not like he was a Republican or something!")

While this is certainly true, it'd be foolish to deny the challenges inherent in interabled conjugality. Financial challenges, emotional challenges, and—yes—physical challenges. No doubt it was a tad bold and naïve of us to trust that love would overcome all differences—if, indeed, differences need overcoming. Now that we're past fifty, M.L. and I can concede that some reflection about how exactly we've managed might prove fruitful. I myself sometimes wonder: Why did she want to tie up her life with mine? And what gave me—a man who depends on round-the-clock personal-care assistance—the chutzpah to imagine, even expect, he could marry and live a normal life like anyone else?

On the other hand, M.L. and I enjoy an undeniable degree of closeness, a give-and-take that other couples might envy. We finish each other's sentences, not always correctly but usually close enough. More than that, we can anticipate each other's moods or reactions to stimuli. She can get me comfortable in my chair when I can't even figure out how to ask or what to ask her for. As for me, well, I can never understand why, in movies, men don't know their wives are pregnant until the wives divulge it like a big secret. Weren't they keeping track of their wives' menstrual cycles? Don't all guys do that, or am I the anomaly? (Probably something in between "all guys" and "only me," but still.)

Is our brand of symbiotic intimacy unique to our in-sync personalities, or could it be a function of our complementary differences, of interabled couplehood in general? Is this, in short, a benefit? (And if so, somebody had better tell those couples who are newly facing disability, before panic and anxiety destroy them!) Did we arrive at it naturally or is it something we've developed and honed over time? And perhaps most crucial of all, can it last?

To shed light on these and other related mysteries, to gain a stronger self-knowledge and advocate for others who may be facing similar questions and judgments, I embark on a quest to zero in on the glue that binds M.L. and me, to study what sticks interabled couples together and perhaps simultaneously give hope to those who are struggling with the mating game. I'll endeavor to accomplish all this through frank conversations with a variety of twosomes at different stages of their romantic lives and from different backgrounds. By coaxing them to share their journeys, I hope to unearth a rich vein of compelling and instructive group-wisdom. My mission, I realize, may reveal something I don't want to see. Like picking at a scab, I might expose lingering insecurities that remain raw and unresolvable. Yet I hope to come out on the other end with not only a better understanding of my own marital bond but also insights into why certain interabled marriages fail while others survive despite—or perhaps because of?—incredible strains.

I'll start with my own marriage to M.L. Then I'll identify other subjects who have something worthwhile to offer and represent a particular perspective. (To be sure, there are plenty of couples in which both members have disabilities, but they're beyond my scope.) Call my survey unscientific and subjective as all get-out, if you like, but I'm certain these discussions will illuminate a broad spectrum of deep-seated truths—and resolve any haunting, personal doubts about whether M.L. and I are a typical interabled union or something unique.

PART I

FIRST COMES LOVE
(AND SEX)

M.L. AND BEN

IT ISN'T THE DA VINCI CODE, but my wedding portrait holds a secret meaning.

For the past quarter century, the unassuming photo has stood on the bookcase in our living room in Los Angeles, in plain view of our sofa. The sofa has changed; the picture has not. It fell to the floor in the earthquake of 1994, shattering its protective glass. We put it back up, glassless.

Yes, displaying a soft-focus eight-by-ten of our beaming younger selves decked out in our finery, glowing in the golden sunlight of a West Hollywood hotel's urban garden, may seem *un*-special—perhaps even the epitome of bourgeois. But for me it conveys a subtle yet important message, hidden in plain sight: there's Mary Lois, radiant in a lacy white cloud, standing beside tuxedoed me . . . in my motorized wheelchair. I'm not propped on a sofa or lounger; my wheelchair is deliberately not cropped out of the photo. It's part of the picture, as it's always been for us.

The point is: we are—and have always been—an interabled couple.

I was born with spinal muscular atrophy, a congenital, progressive, incurable neuromuscular condition. I never walked or stood, and I no longer have the strength to hold or lift a pencil. (I'm writing this with a voice-recognition computer program, and I drive my motorized wheelchair with a hypersensitive lip-controlled mini joystick.) Roughly half the babies born like me don't make it to age two; their hearts and lungs become too weak to go on.

I am now, as I write this, fifty-four years old—"in the first generation to survive to such decrepitude," as my late friend, the writer Harriet McBryde Johnson, who also had SMA, put it in her fine memoir, *Too Late to Die Young: Nearly True Tales from a Life.* (She, alas, didn't make it past fifty.) To look at me today is to see a concentration-camp-thin frame in a Raggedy Ann body, plopped into a state-of-the-art motorized wheelchair. You get used to how I look, or so I'm told. Some people have even said they forget I'm "crippled." That's supposed to be a compliment, I guess. Yet others never see past my obvious deformities. Around me they act what I'll politely term "unnatural."

My wife, M.L., who neither ignores my disability nor acts weird about it, happens to be a couple of years older (not that it's any of your business) and remains what some now call "neuro-typical"—i.e., nondisabled. We've been happily cohabitating for thirty-three years, the past twenty-six of which as legally married. We have two daughters, one in her early twenties and the other still a teenager, both able-bodied.

That's a long time to be an interabled couple. Does Guinness keep records like that?

What we *do* know is that SMA is a broad diagnosis broken up into four types, depending primarily on the age of onset. When I was born, in 1962, it was impossible to diagnose. Nonetheless, my disability became evident when I was about six months old, which is on the early side of SMA type 2. (Type 1 manifests earlier, even at birth; type 3 starts at about eighteen months; and type 4 is "adult onset." Other variations that don't fit these patterns have been discovered too, but I don't really understand them.) At six months, I wasn't sitting up on my own the way my older nondis-abled brother had. When I was put into a seated position, I tended to fall over. Doctors told my parents I'd never be able to cry very loudly because I lacked the necessary breathing capacity. That,

Mom concluded, was the first clue that the doctors didn't know what they were talking about.

To be technical, SMA is a group of genetic disorders with varying degrees of severity. The US National Institutes of Health explains SMA as "a loss of specialized nerve cells, called motor neurons, in the spinal cord and the part of the brain that is connected to the spinal cord (the brainstem). The loss of motor neurons leads to weakness and wasting (atrophy) of muscles used for activities such as crawling, walking, sitting up, and controlling head movement." The latest statistics indicate that one in every six thousand babies is born with some version of SMA. It might not be noticeable at first, as in my case. Symptoms can strike anyone of any race or either gender at any age. Or you might be a carrier and not know it. One in every forty people has the gene, or some 7.5 million Americans. If two of these gene-carriers sprout a child, the kid will also be a carrier and will have a one-in-four chance of developing SMA, which is why my siblings don't have it, though it tends to run in families.

But if one of those parents isn't just a carrier but has SMA, like me, the odds of their kids having it too grow to 50 percent. So if M.L. *were* a carrier, our kids would have a fifty-fifty chance of having my disability.

Everyone who has SMA is different. In my case the progression of the atrophy plateaued when I was about six. That is, the rate at which I continued getting weaker slowed. But, as I learned with great shock and a deep-seated sense of betrayal in my late twenties, the progression never stops completely.

Early on in M.L.'s and my relationship, my disability seemed the least of our differences. I'm a New York–raised Jew; she's a California Protestant. I talked fast; her speech was more considered, full of thoughtful pauses. I tended to be outspoken in my opinions and desires; M.L. would sooner do things than talk about them. She always wanted to have a house with a backyard, but I was a nature-averse city boy. Even our taste in home decor seemed to betray a profound clash: she favored ornate Waterford crystal, because it was from Ireland, as were her ancestors, while I, for no discernible reason, preferred the elegant, clean lines of Steuben.

Our many differences, I think now, were part of the attraction. To me, her particular mix of West Coast free-spiritedness and DAR roots was exotic; to her, my determination must have seemed like a force of nature. (Mom always said my "handicap" shouldn't stop me from pursuing any goal, a principle I took to heart.) Also, M.L. told me later, seeing the no-nonsense way my family assisted me at home helped demystify my limitations and needs. "You weren't aggressive," M.L. recalls now, her brown eyes widening like chocolate ponds behind her antireflective glasses, "but you had a hunger that was sexy. And yet I knew I was safe with you. It was only going to go as far and as fast as I wanted, which was something I needed at the time."

If anything, the novelty of our relationship felt like an asset, not a liability. We figured, in our innocence, why shouldn't we throw in our lots together? As products of the 1960s and '70s, we didn't believe in boundaries. We were all about compromise and acceptance.

Consequently, our glassware and silverware and china patterns and furniture all display eclectic tastes. I learned I was interrupting if I reflexively filled the silences in her natural speech pattern. She learned not to react to every complaint or judgment I uttered, realizing these were little more than a kind of verbal exercise. We live in an apartment with no backyard, but it has a swimming pool and a large terrace in a location that's a compromise between our city and country tastes—Brentwood, one of LA's semisuburban peripheral enclaves.

My disability just seemed a matter of logistics and mechanics. To others, though, it's had a different resonance.

"You're a saint!" M.L. has been told countless times. "I know it must be hard, but good for you for staying with him."

Other strangers have assumed she was my sister or nurse. *No!* we've wanted to scream. My disability is and always has been a part of our romance. It didn't come as a tragic surprise, and we're not together *despite* it. It's simply a part of who I've always been, as much as my race or eye color—and as such, it's part of who we've always been as a couple. It's a strand in the very fabric of our lives together.

All this, we hope, is made plain by the prominently displayed wedding portrait. The picture also comes in handy if M.L. isn't home and some clueless visiting deliveryman or repairman or housecleaner addresses my attendant instead of me, discounting my presence in, well, an unnatural way. I'll try to draw attention to the photo as shorthand for, "Hey, I live here, and I have a life beyond these wheels!"

Rewinding the mental movie of our lives together, I see M.L. and myself on our first dates—talking endlessly during long warm-evening strolls, trying to keep pace with each other though we moved by different means. There was the free Elvis Costello concert in New York. I made M.L. walk thirty blocks through the sweltering stench of Hell's Kitchen in her date shoes and slinky pink dress, because in those days New York buses and taxis weren't yet wheelchair accessible and that was the only way I could get across town. Many catcalls issued forth from the redolent denizens of those mean streets, naturally. Yet, I recall one young guy who smiled stupidly and said, "You two are beautiful."

That was nice, but would he have said the same thing if our handholding weren't across a wheelchair armrest?

Toward the end of the evening, emboldened by a couple of Black Russians, I suggested M.L. ride on my lap. She resisted, but like many disabled people I had learned not to take no for an answer.

"Really," I said. "Climb on. It won't hurt." Whether I meant *it won't hurt ME* or *it won't hurt YOU*, I can no longer recall.

I like to think it was the sheer force of my personality—my gentle, nonthreatening boldness—that made her not only jump onto my lap but fall in love with me. It certainly wasn't the ease with which I move through life.

✦   ✦   ✦

"You were just a kid," M.L. recalls now of our first meeting. I *was* only seventeen, she twenty. She wore her hair in a short boy-cut even then, but there was no mistaking her gender. She'd come to my dad and stepmother Barbara's house in Stamford, Connecticut, to look after my infant half-brother as a summer nanny while on break from college. "I think that's how you got under my radar, in fact, because we were able to become friends and discover shared interests," she adds. Such as Elvis Costello. And a certain holy-profane blend of mixed emotions about religion.

It was the summer before I started my freshman year at Harvard. One year later, Mom died from ovarian cancer. The summer after *that*, when I was nineteen, our friendship shifted gear. That's when M.L. and I started dating. "You went to college, and your mom was dying, and it aged you. You became more of a peer," she recalls. "Then you had the balls to take the first roll of the dice, to ask me out and kiss me!"

If my disability made me seem harmless, an attribute in my favor, M.L. was nevertheless unduly nervous during our first sexual encounters—nervous about injuring me. "Yes," she acknowledges, "with your fragile-looking atrophy, I was worried about balancing in the tiny bed." I had a standard twin, not really built for two. "And if there was a problem, would I have to go get Tom [my attendant at the time]? Or worse, your dad? But you survived the first few encounters; we got more comfortable with each other, and then came the miracle when I was able to lift you!"

It was toward the end of my senior year at Harvard, a month or two before graduation. M.L. was getting a master's in education at nearby Lesley University, and we were already sharing an apartment—a thin-walled, underfurnished two-bedroom in Cambridge, between Harvard Square and Central Square—with my then attendant, Bill. One day, on a desperate whim, she tried lifting me out of my wheelchair and discovered she could! I weighed only about a hundred and twenty pounds, but it was marvelous. It meant that from then on we could go just about anywhere and do anything without having an attendant tag along.

"In fact I *have* hurt you a few times over the years," she reminds me now, with a laugh. It's true. Minor injuries are inevitable when someone else is assisting so much with your physical needs. M.L. says she'll never forget, for example, the morning of our younger daughter's christening. (She'd already had a Hebrew naming ceremony. Remember those mixed feelings about religion? We tried to honor both of our traditions.) The date happened to coincide with M.L.'s fortieth birthday. Her parents and siblings were visiting for the christening, and a big post-ceremony lunch was planned. But while we were getting dressed that morning (M.L. was my only attendant that day, so she had to get *me* dressed too), I was trying to clear my throat and asked her to help me get a good cough. She did, by pressing me forward in my chair to shake up my lungs and compress my diaphragm, which usually worked. This time, however, something snapped. All of a sudden every breath was agony. M.L. and I rushed to the hospital while her parents took care of the girls. "We spent half the day in the ER because I'd 'cracked' your rib," she relates, her voice quivering with uncharacteristic PTSD-like anxiety. She hadn't, actually, cracked anything; it was just strained cartilage. Took six weeks to heal. Almost a funny story now, to me, but apparently that's just me.

Needless to say, the festivities were canceled. We later rejoined the family for pizza in our apartment. Even at that time, I recall trying to shrug the whole incident off with a joke. "We've got to give up that wild sex!" I announced upon returning home from the ER. Fortunately, everyone was desperate for a laugh or I might not have gotten away with it.

The christening finally happened about six months later, to less fanfare.

The intermittent unwelcome remarks from strangers, which still happen today—my all-time favorite was from a homeless guy in Central Park, who saw M.L. riding on my lap and bellowed, "Who says *you* ain't gonna get no pussy?!"—have only drawn us closer. Us against the world!

More than that, though, we've always *felt* closer than other couples. Disability tends to break down the barriers of privacy. If I need to move my arm even an inch, or scratch an itch, I have to ask for help. (And if I get to know you better, I might ask you to blow my nose or assist me in the bathroom!)

Once we learned that M.L. could assist with my daily custodial needs—all of them, including lifting me—we soon decided that having a paid attendant around all the time was too invasive. Especially when so many of the small yet necessary tasks M.L. could do a lot better than the unskilled employees could. So once we moved to LA, away from my family, which in itself was a tremendous leap of faith, we cut back on the attendant hours. No more live-ins, just weekday daytime shifts.

The romantic, rambunctious nocturnal and weekend free-play was great—for about two weeks. Then, predictably, we began to grate on each other's nerves.

"I can't do everything for both of us, you know!" she might snarl. "If you don't like the way I'm doing it, just try to find somebody else who can. Is it ever good enough for you?"

I knew then that I had to budget for additional paid attendant hours (and ask more nicely for the things I needed). M.L. *wanted* to be helpful to me. She's that kind of person. But had I become too accustomed to expecting it? And at what point did having her provide attendanty assistance become a strain on us both? For as overwhelmed as she might occasionally feel, I also could desperately yearn for freedom from her. With an attendant, at least I knew I was in charge.

At first, neither of us could express these frustrations to each other. But honesty has a way of seeping out. Even then, in the heat of the worst grumbling and complaining about each other, we knew we had to work things out. We had to suppress any itch to split up. Separation, at least in the heat of the moment, was unthinkable. If I tried to run away in my electric wheelchair, where would I go (especially in LA, where the geography is vast and I had no other family)? She, in turn, couldn't go storming out either. No matter how angry or trapped she felt, she knew I'd be truly stuck on my own. Worse still, if I said all the venomous things that occasionally seethed through my mind, how could I then turn around and ask her to brush my teeth or put me to bed?

So we had to make up, at least until I was squared away with more helpers. We didn't have to stay in love, but we had to make peace. And as the days became weeks, we were forced to work out our differences. A new love—a more measured, married kind of love, perhaps—eased in.

It took time to work out a reasonable compromise, and to this day the percentage of paid help versus private family time varies depending on the situation. I gradually brought more aides onboard, but not too many. In the meantime, M.L. and I had learned to talk everything out, to be completely honest with each other. The disability forced a degree of intimacy between us that most other couples never know until old age, if then.

When we'd been married a few years and were both in our midthirties, a new priority began filling our lives: the desire for children. Although I'm functionally quadriplegic, I have full sensation from head to toe. I'm fully able to perform sexually, though I can't get on top or move much.

M.L. wanted to get genetic testing to see if she was an SMA carrier. Today there is a simple blood test, and she isn't a carrier. But there was no way to find out in those days.

"If you *are* a carrier, what are you going to do about it?" I asked. "Not have kids? What if my mother had done that?"

Clearly, I felt threatened by the whole idea of genetic testing.

"It's not just about us," she answered. "Is it fair to the child, to have one knowing it might suffer and die before it's two?"

Honestly, I hadn't thought of that. I'd always considered my life pretty good. I had so banished from my mind any thought of how tough it could sometimes be that I never considered how unhappy and frustrated another disabled person might feel. Or how onerous disability can be on parents. Especially if one of the parents can't pull his own weight, literally.

Nonetheless, we decided to take our chances. M.L. yearned to experience pregnancy and didn't want to adopt. I was used to coping with problems and felt that somehow we would be all right. We were a powerful force.

Pregnancy didn't come easily. I had a low sperm count, perhaps from the barrage of childhood X-rays I'd endured, or from sitting all the time, which apparently boils the little critters. In any case, we spent the next four and a half years consulting infertility specialists. We wrestled with whether we could ever be a proper family if we remained childless. It was another battle of us against the world. Familiar territory, to me. I was used to having a body that didn't always cooperate, and I wasn't afraid of medical interventions, if necessary. I was, however, flustered by the emotional fallout, mostly M.L.'s cresting and crashing nerves as each month brought renewed hope followed by crushing disappointment and an ever-worsening bout of near-violent tears.

I joined an infertility support group, but M.L. would never come with me. She still didn't believe in talking about her private troubles. But she drove me to every weekly meeting, dropped me off, and picked me up afterward. This was the kind of compromise we worked out. She didn't have to go, but she wouldn't prevent me from going either.

I'd like to say my hope never waned. That's standard operating procedure for me. But it would be a lie. When at last, after nearly five years, M.L. did become pregnant, her screams of joy could have caused the next California earthquake. For me, however, this meant a new set of special preparations had to be made. I'd need to hire extra help as her belly swelled—help for me that she would become unable to provide. We still didn't want a full-time staff to impinge on our private joy, so I hired a couple of different guys to trade off parts of the day and week. I instituted a system of beepers to summon help in a trice, in those pre-cell-phone days.

(Thanks, Dad and Stepmom, for the financial assistance through this expensive time, and all the others that followed.)

To be frank, I wondered if I'd be able to cope without M.L. to lean on as constantly as I'd grown accustomed to. I wanted to take care of her too, but an important part of that was making sure I could take care of myself. I wanted to be sure that when her water broke, she wouldn't have to worry about looking after me.

I recognize now how ambitious we were. All along, we had to invent so many solutions ourselves—romantic solutions, child-rearing solutions. I could not be the kind of father I'd had, I realized sadly, so I had to create my own ways of connecting, of tending to the kids. And I did. For instance, I couldn't change a diaper, but I made sure I learned how so I could instruct someone else if necessary. And there were things I could do, like give rides on my chair. We strapped a BabyBjörn to the push-handles so I could securely carry each baby, in her time, against my chest as we tooled down the street. When they were bigger, we affixed a strap across the tops of my footrests, making a small seat they could ride on comfortably between my calves. I always watched them in the tub too, singing silly songs and telling stories, ready to holler for M.L. in an emergency (which there never was). I told a lot of stories in those days—Scooby-Doo, X-Men, and fanciful characters such as Gaby the Mongoose—and taught them about how stories work, how they shouldn't worry if the hero's plans don't work out at first. "It's called suspense," I said. "But the third plan *always* works." I taught them how to count to ten, to memorize our home phone number, to use a computer.

I really shouldn't blame other people for misunderstanding us. We were unusual. We were inventing something new—or so we thought. There were few resources to draw on, so I assumed most people born with a severe disability like mine didn't get married at all, let alone have children. (And those who did rarely managed to stay together, I conjectured.)

Our problem was, nobody ever told us we couldn't.

"We faced challenges as they arrived, and survived them," says M.L. now, when I ask her to recall those days, "and we grew in good ways from them. But if we had foreseen them all at once, they would've been too terrifying."

Life is like that, I suppose. You meet challenges as they arise.

"As I've talked to other women my age about their families and others we know," M.L. continues, adjusting her now silver bangs, "I think the same is true for many people. Disability is one part of it, but there are so many kinds of troubles families endure."

I ask her what she'd do differently if she had it to do over again. What advice would present-day M.L. give to herself as a young woman who is considering embarking on a relationship with a disabled young man? "Invest in—" she begins with a sly, alluring chuckle. "No, really, I think I was better off not knowing about the challenges ahead. . . . Perhaps just the knowledge that we're still together, and still best friends as well as spouses, all these years later, would be the nugget to sustain me in those times when it didn't seem possible. And we have two amazing daughters! Who knew?"

Indeed, today we have one daughter in college and the other in high school. When I go to parent events at school, people accept that I belong. I'm not even the only parent in a wheelchair. They may think my disability is a recent phenomenon—that I had a bad diving or skiing accident and severed my spinal cord, or have contracted multiple sclerosis or ALS—but it doesn't matter. We no longer have to explain to anybody why we are together or how we started out. Perhaps we never did. It's our business, not theirs. And we can't control what they think anyway.

Other people still might not get our brand of love, but we know it works. We've proved it. We prove it every day, and we'll keep proving it. And just in case we ever forget what it's all about, there's always the wedding portrait to remind us.

HANNAH AND SHANE

———◆———

IS THIS JUST A FLUKE? If I hadn't met M.L., would I have been alone all these years?

In my darkest moments, that's the root of my lingering whys and wherefores: basic craven insecurity. Strangely, it never occurs to me that, if not for me, she could've been alone. In other words, in my innermost self-doubts, she's desirable and I'm not.

I tell myself, Yeah, but she *did* marry you, Ben. She may have had other boyfriends before you (one that I know of), and might even have had misgivings about being with you, but this is where she stayed. No one forced her.

Logical, this, but it's a hard message to get through my ossified brain. Entrenched uncertainty is a stubborn beast. In time, its nagging, gnarling snarls actually grow almost comfortingly familiar, strangely—a prickly companion. Then I ask myself, Do you think so little of her that you don't believe her when she says she loves you? Certainly not!

"Suddenly I'm not half the man I used to be" goes a well-known lyric. For folks with disabilities, especially progressive conditions like mine, this line can seem like a cruel joke. At any moment you may become less than you were, physically at least. It's inevitable. That doesn't exactly make you a prize catch. "Like what you see?

Well, don't be too surprised if it's gone tomorrow!" Not a recommended pickup line.

Beyond this raw, animal self-pity, for many lonely people, lies simple, old-fashioned horniness. In some corners, that's the underlying message of the disability rights movement today: "We are sexual beings! Love us. Fuck us." Many terrific young disabled folks—of all genders and orientations—feel not merely rejected but utterly overlooked in our sexed-up culture. And they're not wrong to want equal opportunity in . . . all things. We veterans of the movement may be more concerned about big-picture issues such as affordable accessible housing, long-term home-based personal-care assistance, inequities in the workplace, and other measures of social justice. But for many crips, especially the younger ones, the burning question is, "How do I hook up?" or (more politely), "Will I ever find love?"

Perhaps it's a case of putting the cart before the horse: better jobs and better long-term-care financing and social justice would surely increase our conjugal capital and make us more sought after. Still, in the meantime, the longing to get laid is a red-blooded expression of a tremendous leaden loneliness.

To gain a sense of the current romantic and erotic climate for young adults with disabilities, I talk to Shane Burcaw, the twenty-three-year-old blogger and author of the young-adult memoir *Laughing at My Nightmare*, and his girlfriend, Hannah Aylward, twenty, a sophomore at Carleton College in Northfield, Minnesota. Shane uses a motorized wheelchair, in which he sits leaning far to his right, his beige-ski-cap-clad head precariously balanced while his rib cage supports the weight of his upper body. His body doesn't amount to much weight, though. Shane weighs just sixty-four pounds. His arms and legs are toothpicks. You know this because he's not afraid to wear shorts and T-shirts in the summer (yes, even with the ski cap), an unselfconscious boldness I privately admire. You could also know it by reading his book or his blog of the same name, which are full of candid photos.

Here's how he describes himself in *Laughing at My Nightmare*:

> Because of a neuromuscular disease I've had since birth, my arms
> and legs are slightly fatter than a hot dog. My elbows and wrists
> are extremely atrophied; they look exactly like Tyrannosaurus
> Rex arms when I hold them against my chest. I am a few inches
> shy of five feet, and when I sit in my chair, it seems like I'm even
> shorter. My head is normal human size, which looks ridiculously
> funny/creepy sitting on top of my tiny body. Imagine a bobble-
> head doll in a wheelchair. I don't even blame people for staring.
> If I were a stranger, I would probably stare at me, too.

Like me, Shane was born with SMA type 2. He never walked
and gradually but steadily lost the use of his muscles. His T. rex
arms appear short—or rather, hopelessly bent at the elbows and
wrists, his fingers curled inward. One leg is shorter than the other,
but that's not because of SMA. As a kid, he tried to play soccer in
his wheelchair and ended up on the ground with a broken bone
that never healed right. He lives at home with his middle-class
parents and younger, nondisabled brother, Andrew, in suburban
Pennsylvania.

He freely refers to SMA as a "disease," which is not a term most
disability rights activists like to embrace. He's keenly aware of its
toll on him and of the insecurity of his having much of a future
at all. Yet he's not gloomy in his disposition. He prefers to find
humor in every situation.

We first speak in March 2014, when he's twenty-two. We connect on Skype, because travel is difficult for both of us. Occasionally, his words come with difficulty—physical difficulty, not
mental difficulty. He's quick-witted, but his voice sounds a little
tight and breathy at times as he struggles to articulate and project. (Hell, mine does too sometimes.) He's learned to manage
his speech so well, however, that I quickly became rapt. It's not
just the content of his words but the hip patter he's developed.

You're never quite sure if he's serious or joking, and if I had to bet I'd say the latter.

Some time ago he began expressing that humor online, on Tumblr. No sugarcoating, though. He's shockingly frank about his limitations and frustrations. He freely addresses readers' questions such as "How do you poop?" with unabashed honesty, describing how his father or brother lifts him over the toilet and wipes him afterward. He illustrates this with a humorous photograph, which I suspect is staged. On his brother's birthday, he posted: "the happiest of birthdays to the kid who has been helping me pee all these years."

But until recently, he thought he would never have a girlfriend.

"Two or three years ago, I had never had a romantic relationship," he tells me. "I grew up with tons of friends, and lots of them were female. But it would never go any further than that. I never pushed it with any of them because I didn't want to hurt relationships that were already perfectly good. So at that point I was just kind of like, maybe I just won't have a girlfriend. Ever."

At that I hold my breath. Perhaps he senses the lump in my throat.

"I didn't think too much about it," he says then, "but it upset me *if* I thought about it."

Shane is palpably aware of the steady progression of his SMA—not daily, to be sure, but unavoidably. I confess that, at first, I was turned off by his blog and book's implications. The very idea of "my nightmare" doesn't seem to serve the cause of greater disability inclusion. Don't we want to get away from pity mongering? Isn't he pandering to the popular imperative that people with disabilities should be inspirational? But now that I've gotten to know him and his work better, I've had a change of heart. Maybe he's actually turning the stereotype on its head. What's that old philosophy about how accurately naming something removes its power? By turning his circus spotlight on that nightmare stereotype, he's helping lift the mystery and fear.

Shane's charm is overpowering. Without pausing, he breezily informs me that everything changed for him romantically after his blog got going. It's fair to say that Shane practically lives in his blog. For people with mobility impairments, the computer can be like a passport to the world. And you can visit incognito—no one need know about your disability, or at least about the extent of it, or about what you look like, how you talk, how you breathe, and how you eat, all of which can be labored for someone like Shane. Perhaps if I were a young single man today, that's how I'd meet women.

But he doesn't hide behind his online persona. In fact, his blog is downright narcissistic. Besides the uplifting yet scatological discourses on his life, he posts photos and videos of himself almost daily. He isn't afraid to look foolish. He's perfected a gobsmacked, slack-mouthed, wide-eyed shocked expression. And the attention he's garnered has led him to create his own nonprofit, Laughing At My Nightmare Inc., to raise awareness of SMA and solicit funds for those who can't afford wheelchairs, vans, and other necessary equipment. He gives talks in his reedy, comically clipped voice to school groups and clubs explaining his mission and soliciting donations.

Holding nothing back is part of the magic of Shane's message. He's able to shape the way his disability and his life experiences are presented, and he does so with self-aware, unsentimental, unabashed gusto.

"Two or three years ago I got an e-mail from this girl who said, 'Hey, I read your blog and I love it,'" he explains to me. "I kind of rolled my eyes like I do whenever I get one of those e-mails, but she mentioned she was local [and] would really love to hang out."

Shane's expectations were muted, tempered by experience. "There was no suggestion of anything [more] at that point," he continues. "So honestly, just for the hell of it, I sent her my number and said, 'Hey, let's text. That'd be fun.'. . . I didn't even think about it. Just did it and moved on."

What developed was a virtual friendship, conducted entirely online and by phone. "We texted back and forth," he says, "and a few days later we started talking about relationships, and I described to her my whole difficulty with having a girlfriend because I rely on other people so much. That's kind of a turnoff for most young people. At least [that's] the way I've experienced it. And she came back and was very forward about it. She just said, 'Honestly, all of that means nothing to me. I would love to get to know you on a deeper level.' So she came over and we hung out."

The friendship stayed platonic over several more visits—she always visiting him, at his parents' house, because he lacked independent mobility. His family did, however, allow him a high degree of privacy. It wasn't unusual for Shane to spend hours in his bedroom on his own with his computer, so why not leave him alone in his room with a visiting friend?

Even when talk with that friend turned to kissing and more.

"The first time I taught her how to lift me, that was, like, a big step in the relationship! She was nervous, but she wanted to try it, because we couldn't really be intimate with me sitting in the wheelchair," says Shane. "So I told her it's fairly easy. I don't weigh that much. I kind of assessed that she was fit enough to be able to do it. [It's] something I have to think about when I'm talking to new people. I immediately size up if they'll be able to lift me. I don't have any type of lift device or anything."

For me, it's interesting to contemplate this particular disability perspective. Most of us might size up potential dates by their smile or figure. Shane has to gauge their weight-lifting ability!

I ask him if this girlfriend had any previous experience with people with disabilities. "None at all," he responds. "She was in one relationship before me. But no one who had a disability."

Though it was a new experience for both of them, in different ways, they managed. Honesty, open-mindedness, patience, and perseverance got them through. "We were able to be intimate once I was out of my chair," Shane continues. "I was nineteen, and that was the most amazing experience of my life. It was different [for her], obviously, but she didn't mind it. I was able to do enough on my own that it worked out."

He can touch and kiss, but he can't hump or grind or climb on top or assume exotic positions. He describes sex graphically in his book—oral, manual, etc. "Having a real human girl to share this kind of intimacy with was surreal," he writes.

Things progressed from there. "The texting and Skyping were constant, but it just didn't compare to the physical intimacy. . . . A few weeks later I asked her to be my girlfriend, feeling like it was the natural progression of our relationship," he tells me.

That's not the end of Shane's story. As if in answer to my unspoken question, Shane then informs me that, in the end, good sex wasn't enough. "A few months later," he goes on, "I was thinking about us, and I realized I didn't really *connect* with her. The only reason I'd jumped on being with her was she was the first person who expected anything more than friendship with me. But then again, I didn't want to break up with her if I was never going to find someone else. I didn't know if she was, like, an oddball. . . . At first I lied to myself and said, 'Oh yeah, it's much deeper.' But over time I had to admit she wasn't a person I enjoyed being around. So I had to let her go."

He puts it a tad more specifically in his book: "I suddenly felt like I was only interested because of the amazing orgasms I was getting."

To me he says his "conscience wouldn't allow me to be with her if it was only for the physical stuff," which strikes me as a mature observation for a guy who was at the time only nineteen. "She understood I was young and inexperienced and didn't really know what I wanted yet," he reflects, adding that they still talk occasionally. They're still friends.

Jill was twenty-two, three years older than Shane. I begin to wonder if age difference is a key element to interabled attraction. After all, M.L. is also three years older than I am. But that age-difference idea shifts with what Shane says next. "My second relationship was kind of the opposite," he volunteers with a laugh.

On his blog, he'd requested volunteers for a video project. "I selected a girl from Florida, and, really, it was completely business," he explains. "We worked together that summer from a distance. She stayed in Florida. We worked via Skype and texting and e-mail and all that."

Shannon was only eighteen; Shane was now twenty. Working together, they became close friends. "Probably my best friend at that time [though] we hadn't actually met in person."

Even after the video project was done, they kept in touch. "We Skyped nearly every night, and it got to a point where we admitted we liked each other as more than friends," recalls Shane. "But because of the distance and some hesitations she had about my disability, she just finally said, 'I'm not ready to be in a relationship yet, so let's just hold off.' It hurt but I understood, and I didn't want to push her."

Then came a Christmas surprise. "In December, I was in my bedroom, and my brother was home for the holidays, and he said, 'Hey, my friend is coming over tonight, just so you know.' He was being a little weird. Then Shannon comes walking in! She had planned this with my family, to come visit for Christmas. I didn't know. It blew my mind! So we spent the next four days together, which was awesome. But still just as very close best friends.

"Then she went home, but she came back for spring break. That time she stayed for a week, during which we kissed for the first time. It was a big moment. But still . . . she'd lost her mom to cancer when she was fourteen, and she didn't want to fall in love with someone who might up and die. I understood. I can't say, 'I guarantee nothing will happen to me.' 'Cause, you know, I could get sick tomorrow and that could be the end. It's tough. It was probably the toughest part of that relationship."

Or at least up until that point. Tougher moments lay ahead but not without interludes of sublimity. "That summer she was here for a whole month," says Shane. "And that's when she finally said, 'You know what? I've forgotten my reasons for wanting to hold off on the relationship. So let's just do it.' So we made it official."

The next eight months were "seriously the best time of my entire life," he tells me. "She came up here once a month. . . . I taught her how to lift me, and we were able to be intimate. So that was cool."

Cool though it may have been, there was soon trouble in paradise. "We had our fair share of problems," Shane acknowledges. First, there were mobility/transportation inequities. "Sometimes she'd say, 'I'm giving up so much of my life to be with you. I know it's not your fault, but you never come down to Florida.' And I'm like, 'It's just difficult.' And she'd say, 'I want someone who can be here for me and help me and hold me.' Stuff like that."

Shane pauses then. He swallows audibly. "That was really tough," he continues. "We both knew there was nothing [we could do about it]. It wasn't anybody's fault. It was just the way things were."

How exactly they dealt with these differences, he can't specify. It's a case of "if there's a will . . ." "We always found a way to work through it," says Shane with characteristic casualness. "We had our moments where, intimately, I wasn't able to do everything as good as an able-bodied person might. So we had our late-night fights where I'm apologizing and she's telling me not to apologize, but I feel bad and she's saying, 'Don't feel bad,' but she's obviously upset. That kind of sucked. But we got through it."

Perhaps when you're used to getting by, doing without, compromising, these sorts of limitations don't seem so catastrophic. Shannon might not have felt so blasé about the physical limitations, but Shane's determination and desire were more than sufficient to make up the difference. In his book, he writes: "All I know for sure is that if life goes the way I *want* it to, Shannon . . . will be the girl I spend the rest of my life with. It excites me to share that with the world in such a permanent way."

Ah, young love! Young hyperbole! To me he allows, "I'd never loved someone as much as I loved her. And I think she'd say the same about me."

But they *were* still very young, and happily ever after it wasn't.

Like many romantic schisms, the reasons for their eventual split aren't exactly clear. Or maybe they're entirely too clear. Telling me about it, Shane struggles for the right words, but his meaning rings out like breaking glass. "For a while, she was planning on moving up here to be with me, to help out with all my stuff," he says. "She wanted to be the one that takes care of me. And for an eighteen- or nineteen-year-old to be committing her life like that, it's not practical. When she asked me for the breakup, I was upset, obviously, but I knew it was the right thing to do. I can't expect her to give up her life for me at this point in *her* life."

I ask Shane the question he seems to have been hinting at: Did she get flak from her family or friends for bedding a cripple?

"Yes," he answers without skipping a beat. "That was another thing. Three or four months into the relationship, she started telling me about how her sister and the woman they live with [a close family friend/guardian] didn't really agree with her being with me. I've met them, and they're not evil people. But once, the woman said something like, 'She's not going to be able to take care of you and provide for you!' Her aunt was also kind of against it and didn't really understand what she saw in me, because of the wheelchair. It made Shannon so mad. She was livid at them. But being around them all the time kind of changed her mind. Their thoughts slipped in more and more. She started to understand and even agree with their perspective."

There was peer pressure as well. "Her sister has an able-bodied boyfriend, and they're always running around, going out, drinking, having sex, the way normal young people do," he says. "She doesn't want to be shallow, but she sees this and feels like she's missing out. I want to be able to give her those experiences."

If he means he also wishes he could have those experiences himself, he doesn't let on. It's not obvious to me why he can't go out partying and drinking, but there's a hint in his book, a story about a time he stayed out late with a friend and drank too much. His friend passed out, and there was no one to help him call home, lie down, or even go to the bathroom till morning. To me, these seem solvable problems. I don't know why he's so fully dependent on his family, why he's hesitant to hire help. It's not just a financial matter for him. In his book, he envisions an over-weight, overbearing nurse who would boss him around, and he rejects the whole idea. It's as if going too far outside his comfort zone sounds too dangerous, which I understand, to a point. It's a little like an old person who's afraid of getting knocked down on the street and so prefers to stay home. Disability doesn't let you be careless or spontaneous. With a condition like Shane's, poor planning or devil-may-care heedlessness can be tantamount to drinking Comet. Still, you've got to take risks. It's key to independence.

I don't lecture him. Instead, I ask, "Do you think dealing with a disability makes you see the world and face things in a way that other people don't until they're much older?"

He has, so far, never paused to answer a question, and this time is no exception. "My whole life I've lived with the knowledge that I will be worse physically in ten years than I am today. That's always the case," he says flatly. "Ever since I was in middle school, I've been pushing myself to do everything now, now, now, instead of down the road."

Where relationships are concerned, he observes, he might come across as being in a rush to marry. A certain urgency per-meates his life. When you feel as if you're living on borrowed time, you can't let a relationship develop and mature too slowly. "I never said anything to either girlfriend about marriage or kids or anything like that, but I guess I give off a certain vibe," he chuckles, and I remember that declaration of everlasting love in his book. "I want to settle down and do stuff I'm afraid I won't be able to do, ever. So even though we never explicitly discussed it, and Shannon never said that was a problem, it probably was."

Then Shane surprises me with an about-face: "I do plan on getting married, having kids, all that fun stuff. I mean, don't ask me *how* that will work." He concedes the big unknowns could scare anyone away, especially someone "who is trying to figure out her own life."

Nine months after our initial conversation, his romantic life changed again. He met Anna when she attended a talk he gave at the University of Connecticut. "Our personalities clicked," he recalls in a separate interview. In a matter of weeks he asked her to be his "official" girlfriend, and she said yes. "Anna was more mature than anyone I'd been in a relationship with before. Communication was a huge part of it," he says. If something was bugging either one of them, they weren't "afraid to say, 'This needs to change' or 'Let's try doing this a different way,'" he says.

During her summer break from college, they took a weekend trip together, just the two of them. Anna took over all of his personal-care tasks, which include inserting a feeding tube into his nose at night, to fill his belly with needed nutrients and calories. None of these tasks could have been a surprise, since he describes them in detail in his blog and book. Around that time he posted this: "This morning Anna picked boogers out of my nose with a pair of tweezers, so if she's not The One, I'm not sure who is."

It's the very definition of caregiving, sure, but isn't this also a kind of intimacy?

But in the fall Anna went back to school, and Shane was still living in his parents' house. By and by, the relationship fizzled. "It wasn't making us happy anymore, so I ended it," he reflects. Nearly a year passed before he found Hannah—his fourth "official" girlfriend, and he's only twenty-four!—or should I say, she found him. Via his blog.

"After reading for a few hours, I was sufficiently smitten to e-mail him," Hannah tells me. She's tall, with long golden-brown hair and a swimmer's broad shoulders. She liked Shane's sense of humor and approach to life, and boldly ended her e-mail with: "PS: I think you're cute." She smiles brightly. "We FaceTimed that same day."

As of this writing, they've only been together about two months. "Hannah has quickly learned all the intricacies of helping me," says Shane. "Although we may appear an unlikely couple, we've found that the obstacles that ostensibly separate us are quite easily overcome with laughter, dedication, and love." He jokes that they plan to marry quickly so there's a contractual obligation to make it last. "Sometimes I fall into funks where I get down on myself, thinking my disease will make Hannah's life too hard," he concedes. "But it's important to remember she wouldn't be with me if she didn't want to be. No one is forcing her, so if she says she's happy, she is. It's important to listen to your partner."

Perhaps it'd be a good idea for me to take Shane's advice myself and remember that if M.L. weren't truly happy with me, she wouldn't have stuck around, disability or not.

Later, thinking back over all this, I consider how I ought to know better than to wonder how Shane keeps going. People wonder that about me all the time, seeing me in my wheelchair, watching as I'm fed in restaurants, and so forth. Shane and I keep going because we have no alternative. Nevertheless, I ask Shane to reflect on what fuels him. Perhaps the messages he received from his parents, I suggest.

"They never said, 'You won't do anything,'" he responds. "They live on the belief that I'm going to live to be a hundred! Now, whether they just say that for my sake or not, they've always treated me like my life would be as normal as I wanted it to be. And I think it's great. You know, I don't think it should be any other way!"

I agree. Parental expectations can so often become self-fulfilling prophecies. I've noticed a trend when I talk to those lonely, horny disabled people who are desperate to get laid. Invariably their parents saddled them with the dire belief, the bleak certitude, that they would be alone forever. And so it happens.

Yet I'm also heartened to confirm what I already knew—namely, that some people *are* open-minded, that having a severe disability isn't necessarily a romantic or sexual nonstarter these days. No one knows better than crips that perseverance pays off, and apparently that adage is true in love too.

WANDA AND KEVIN

THE NEXT PHASE for many developing romances is the big M. Just thinking about it can spark comment from, well, the whole tribe. Parents, siblings, aunts, and uncles of both spouses. Then come civic or religious leaders, assorted caterers, florists, photographers, dressmakers. Everybody can weigh in. The relationship abruptly becomes public and, therefore, fair game.

I never had too much trouble in this regard. M.L. and I had already been living together for six years, so just about everyone we knew was already used to our couplehood. I do, however, remember when my future father-in-law asked, in all innocence, "Why get married? You're already as good as married."

But there *is* a difference, a vague desire to fit into a pattern that heretofore seemed fusty, alien, outdated. And, alas, his wasn't the only question raised about our plans. Not the details of our wedding plans, to be clear, so much as our very desire to even consider tying the knot.

To gauge the current milieu in which interabled pairings take place, I talk to Wanda, a nondisabled thirty-year-old with a PhD, currently an assistant professor of sociology in suburban Tennessee, and her fiancé, Kevin, a twenty-six-year-old student in Georgia with—you guessed it—SMA. (These are not their real names, and certain other identifying traits have been changed; the couple requested anonymity.)

"We met through eHarmony," Kevin tells me, by e-mail. He's shy about speaking. His disability affects every muscle in his body, including those that control his lungs, jaw, and voice. I see in pictures that he's thin with atrophy, though not as petite as Shane. It strikes me that Internet dating sites are probably full of people with disabilities. They can pretend to be anybody, control the message. Spinning your persona to give an idealized first impression is de rigueur for everyone, disabled or not, on dating sites, isn't it?

In his high-backed powered wheelchair, Kevin sits up straight, looking comfortably casual in a loose-fitting aqua-colored T-shirt. He has closely shaved hair and a slight beard. His smile is warm and relaxed. From his photo, you might not fully cotton to the scope of his limitations.

"Kevin was not a match for me because I placed high importance on height," explains Wanda, with a self-conscious giggle, during our first phone chat. She's not shy about speaking. Her voice carries the passion of someone on the defensive, I note, yet it's a defensiveness mixed with optimism. I picture her as a sturdy, powerful woman with professorial glasses, but at this point I don't actually know what she looks like. When I do get to see her, I get a slightly different impression. She's strong all right, but she seems playful and far from harsh, with long lustrous black hair that cascades past her shoulders. No glasses.

She reassures me that she soon got over the height restriction after she and Kevin chatted online. They had an almost instant intellectual, spiritual connection. She knew he had a disability—she could hear it in his voice, if nothing else—but that in itself wasn't a turnoff. They quickly arranged to meet.

She had to drive four or five hours to see him on his own territory. As in Shane's case, he didn't have transportation options. That didn't bother her either, says Wanda now. But something else did.

"When I first met him in person, I was very much taken aback," she confides. I appreciate her candor and ask her why. Sure, she says, she'd known he had a disability and used a wheelchair. She just hadn't realized from his eHarmony posting, Facebook pictures, or daily Skype video chats exactly how thin and weak he was from the neck down. "On Skype, I only saw him from the shoulders up. I never saw how affected his arms are. I mean, it was really awkward at the beginning, because I was always way back from the camera and he never was. I thought, maybe he thinks I'm crazy or creepy for not approaching the camera or wanting to see more of him [physically]," she recalls. "But we connected so well, talking about things that we really have in common, like values."

She'd had limited prior experience with people with disabilities. "During middle school, I hung out with some kids with disabilities because they ate lunch near the orchestra room, where I hung out a lot," she says.

Wanda's friends told her to be honest, not to lead Kevin on, to tell him about her misgivings. Which she did, in time. She'd had relationships before, one of which she describes as abusive, and a failed marriage. So she knew to be careful with her emotions, but she couldn't get over how close she felt when she talked with Kevin.

"What helped with my initial discomfort was that it caused us to have a conversation about it," she observes. "I was like, 'Hey Kevin, I don't know if I'm okay with your disability.' A lot of our early conversations involved, 'I don't know enough about you. I'm still learning.' He seemed okay with that, but he was doing his best not to overwhelm me."

Actually, Kevin, who had no prior amorous experiences at all, had tried to hide his limitations, to minimize certain aspects of his disability—the most unpleasant, scariest effects of his muscle weakness. She describes the head-falling-over business. "His head just falls back sometimes, like when he moves forward too fast, because his neck can't hold his head up," she explains. "He then has to speed up and stop real fast" to propel his head forward to an upright position. "The physics of it is amazing," Wanda says. "The jarring motion flings his head forward just enough."

She almost sounds like a clinical observer of a foreign species. She means no offense, I'm sure, though she admits she was "not quite okay" with Kevin's "disabled moments," as he euphemistically calls them. They are no doubt more numerous than that phrase implies. "I wasn't making a decision one way or the other," she adds. "I just knew there were certain things I was not okay with."

Nevertheless, every few weeks for the next several months she made the long trip to meet him on his home turf. It wasn't for sex, at least not at first, she tells me. They simply enjoyed each other's company. "We didn't get that physically intimate until, oh, five months after our initial meeting," she insists. Wanda squarely attributes her sexual hesitancy to his disability, not his personality. And it was her resistance, not his, that caused them to delay intercourse. Kevin's disability doesn't affect his sexual functioning; he just doesn't have the muscles to move his body, to get on top.

What thawed Wanda's libido was a Christmas visit with her family in California. "After that, I made the decision I would be okay with his disability," she recalls.

What happened to induce her to take the plunge? It was partly an act of defiance, of rebellion at her mother's negative reaction. "When I first mentioned Kevin to my mom, her reaction was, *Wow!* Then she used her heart condition—she has heart disease—to say, 'You know, you're going to give me a heart attack!'"

Hearing this part of Wanda and Kevin's story, I think of M.L.'s mother. She's never been anything but kind. But during M.L.'s and my first year living together, there was an evening when M.L. came downstairs to our basement bedroom in Dad and Barbara's house in Connecticut with a rheumy glint in her eyes. I asked what was wrong.

"Nothing," she said. "Just got off the phone with my mom."

I had only met M.L.'s mother once at that point, in a sort of drive-by visit when we still lived in Cambridge. I'd liked her but couldn't break through the special bond that enveloped their relationship like a San Francisco fog. They even had their own language, it seemed to me.

"How's she?" I asked, trying to exude innocent curiosity. In memory, I was lying in our queen-size bed, naked under the covers, and she was still dressed, waiting for the bathroom. It was often that way—the attendant would get me ready for bed first, then vanish so M.L. could strip down. I think now that I thought of my future mother-in-law as a rival—not for M.L.'s affections so much as for her attentions. M.L. was still very much the good girl who sought maternal approval. "What'd you talk about?"

"You, actually. She likes you and asked about you."

I sensed there was something more. There was.

"But at the end of the conversation," M.L. continued, "she said, 'Oh honey, why can't you find someone else?'"

A sour, sludgy bitterness erupted within me, traveling from gut to heart to head. I tried to wish it away, to decontaminate. I said something like "Oh?" with (I hope) a certain practiced, artificial evenhandedness. My goal that night, after all, was to be closer with M.L., not confront her, to watch her undress and welcome her under the covers. Then I said, "I don't like that, but I can't really blame her. What'd you say back?"

"You have to understand my mother," was her answer. "This is all new to her."

Not what I was hoping for. I wanted moral outrage. I wanted her advocacy. But I couldn't yet determine if this was going to be a big deal. Was her mother's disapproval in earnest? Was this a red flag warning of something that could ultimately destroy our romance? It was circa 1984, and we were still on shaky ground, both pretty insecure about our futures.

Two decades later—feeling safer, more secure, and more self-assured—I obliquely referred to M.L.'s mother's early unease in an NPR commentary on *Morning Edition*. I said that my future mother-in-law had "expressed concern" to M.L. but that we were now good friends. After the broadcast my mother-in-law e-mailed me, apologized, and said she was glad we were now friends. And so we are.

Unlike my situation, Wanda's parental disapproval was nothing short of an ordeal. She describes "a series of talks . . . like a three-step intervention." The first step came during a long walk with her father. He "proceeded to tell me the story of this overweight lady who was able to find a husband *who was physically able*, and they had children, and how her husband loved her *despite her being overweight*. I'm not kidding you!" says Wanda, adding, "I *am* overweight. But by their standards I'd be too heavy if I was anything over size zero! I mean, in college I was a size six or eight and ran in the LA Marathon. But if you asked them, I was morbidly obese even then!"

In Wanda's family, her weight was directly linked to the type of mate she could hope to land. To Wanda herself, though, her parents' attitude was a lifelong source of shame and spirit-crushing insecurity. Is it any wonder that she was drawn to a man who accepted her as she was? "It was very painful. Growing up I had a lot of self-doubt," she says. "My dad is retired from the Air Force and US Postal Service, so he can come across as very authoritative."

The second step in the intervention was taken by Wanda's sister. You can practically hear Wanda's eyes rolling as she mocks her sister's voice; even many months later, Wanda can barely contain her irritation. "She pulled me aside and gave me this whole, 'I don't know if you've considered the burden you're putting upon us by being with this man,'" relates Wanda.

A final volley was discharged by a united front: her mom and dad together. "They literally cornered me in the living room. I had to jump over the coffee table to escape!" she says with a loud sigh. "This was the first time I actually had to tell them, repeatedly and emphatically, 'You have to accept me. It's as simple as that.'"

Hearing this, something uncomfortable occurs to me. Wanda is of Asian descent; Kevin is African American. Was there a racial component to Wanda's parents' objection? I ask.

"I've never dated within my own culture before," she answers. "So this wasn't the first time my parents had come down on me about my choice in men. But it was the first time I actually had to stand my ground."

In other words, the ethnic difference wasn't new or shocking to her parents. It was Kevin's disability that really got her family's goat.

Even now, these encounters with her family leave Wanda questioning her motives like a postulant searching for eternal truths. She is self-aware enough to reconsider the situation from all angles. She e-mails me a numbered list, as if her relationship were a matter for the head and not the heart. A true academic, she is trying to break the problem into quantifiable parts:

Essential aspects of my thought process to be in a committed relationship with Kevin:

1. *The decision to date him without being pushed towards him because of alienation from my family*
2. *The decision to date him without being pulled towards him because of interest in his special condition*
3. *Deciding to date him despite mixed messages from family and friends*
4. *"Artificial bond" that might exist because of my need to take care of him and his need for someone able-bodied to help him*
5. *My need and desire to be useful, giving me an outlet for my engineering ingenuity and creativity*

Call me a narcissist, but I'm struck by how Wanda's thought process echoes some of my own bone-deep insecurities. Everything she observes about her motivations I could ascribe to M.L.

at some point in our lives. Her "engineering ingenuity," for example, is certainly a quality they have in common. Even before we were dating, M.L. was offering to fix the headrest on my wheelchair or make me a new one with her sewing machine. I recall that I rebuffed such attentions at first, not wanting to get her involved in my problems. But in the end I couldn't resist her innate understanding of what I needed. It turned out to be good for both of us.

Wanda's carefully formulated self-doubts don't dissuade her. She concludes that, despite her father's innuendo, she isn't settling for a man whom only a desperate woman could love. Yet other hurdles await them.

Kevin, she says, receives Medicaid to help pay for his attendant. Apparently he's not allowed to go out of state overnight with the attendant—to visit Wanda, for instance—without risking losing benefits. This is a problem with many state-sponsored benefits programs. Personal assistants are supposed to provide so-called home health care, which may include trips to doctors and grocery stores but not overnight visits out of state. Advocates have tried to overturn these circumscriptions, with mixed results. But many folks tell me they pay no attention to such absurd constraints. After all, who's going to report them?

Still, fear of jeopardizing needed benefits can run deep. Just the threat of losing even an ounce of custodial support causes righteous outrage and justified panic. In this as in so many cases, the boundaries and stipulations are woefully out of date. They make independence conditional. In Kevin's case, he has a wheelchair-accessible van but isn't able to drive it himself. So he can't visit Wanda on his own.

Often, however, when she comes to visit, they don't really want the attendant around. In fact, some of the best times are when the attendant is off. I can't help thinking they're discovering what M.L. and I learned years ago: the advantages of the extra help are often trumped by the disadvantages of having another personality around. On the other hand, the price of privacy is that the able-bodied partner may have to fill in as helper. It's a never-ending trade-off.

I'm reminded of an old stand-up routine about how you might pick up a sex partner at a bar and do God knows what to each other's bodies all night long, yet in the morning the thought of sharing a toothbrush is too gross to bear. That's sort of what it can feel like to provide attendant assistance. Smooch and fondle and whatnot, but to provide basic custodial help in the bathroom feels odd, unromantic, inappropriate.

I ask Wanda about this. "I stop at wiping his butthole," she tells me. "That is the one thing I won't do if I don't have to. However, I'm always worried that someone else won't do a good enough job."

Boy, can I relate! After M.L. made that first new headrest, she began doing more and more. Shaving me, adjusting the positions of my fingers. At that point I gladly accepted (not that I could've stopped her if I'd tried; she was never satisfied with the way my attendants shaved me or washed between my toes, among other things). It's just easier to explain what you need to someone who loves you—someone who's helping because she cares—as opposed to someone who's paid to listen. And someone who cares will always do a better job than someone who's just in it for pay (especially considering how little personal-care assistants are usually paid).

Nevertheless, having a lover be one's caregiver isn't exactly ideal either. It can take a toll on the able-bodied partner and rob the disabled person of a feeling of autonomy. Relying on a paid attendant you direct yourself is the closest many disabled folks can come to being self-reliant. Most of all, it can strain the romance, the mystery.

In a subsequent interview, Wanda elaborates. She says that whether and how much she should help Kevin with basic custodial tasks is the subject of ongoing discussion. "One of the things we constantly have to discuss is, well, he's really good about making sure it doesn't become burdensome on me. Like, you know, he'll say, 'You seem very tired.' I might have to put him in bed or whatever, but I'd rather have that—that degree of closeness and privacy—than not be comfortable enough to walk around in my underwear, if you will."

It's a constant balancing act, as I said before: privacy versus making sure both partners' physical and emotional needs are met.

"I generally don't get her to help with bathroom duties or transfers, unless we just want to be alone without an attendant," volunteers Kevin, adding, "but ever since the first day we met, it's as if she instinctively understood my subtle limitations. For instance, she knows to lay things out on the table or in bed or wherever so they're close within my reach."

Kevin tells a story via e-mail that illustrates a compelling counterpoint: a disabling condition—or "moment," as he might put it—can actually bring a couple closer. Like a magnet, if it doesn't repulse, it draws in. "On our third date, I puked my guts out and was hospitalized for diabetic ketoacidosis caused by my body not absorbing insulin. I'm diabetic," he writes. (This has nothing to do with his SMA. It seems that many of us who have a disability often have multiple disabilities. Just lucky, I guess.) "It was such a terrible day in some ways, but it will give us something to talk about for years to come and was a bonding experience. We coped with the crisis together, and afterward laughed about it."

Doesn't sound like my idea of a fun date, but if puking your guts out and being hospitalized doesn't sink the relationship, I suppose nothing will. It's like the Nietzschean bromide that what doesn't kill you makes you stronger. Perhaps such near misses make a couple stronger too.

Whether or not the puking episode became part of her motivation, Wanda has grown single-minded in her pursuit of making their union a success. She has to, considering the barbed-wire hoops they're being made to jump through. She tells me she recently sought genetic testing to determine if she's one of the one-in-forty who carries the SMA gene. If she and Kevin both carry the gene, their children would have a fifty-fifty chance of having SMA. But even this sensible pursuit has been waylaid by unnecessary obstacles. To date, three different doctors have refused to conduct the simple blood test.

"I explained that I'm trying to be responsible. I told them I'm dating a man with SMA. Their response is always disbelief—'You plan on having children with him?' Because I don't have a sibling or parent with the condition and was not yet married, I don't have what qualifies as a 'relationship with someone with SMA,' so testing me doesn't qualify as a medical necessity for insurance purposes," she thunders.

Listening to her explain it, you can't help but take in her irritation. If this were a cartoon, there'd be steam billowing out of her ears. I'm almost thankful there was no test available when M.L. and I first played with the idea of making babies. She did have one later, though, after our first daughter was born, just to be prepared for any eventuality. (Again, she is not a carrier.) I recall the tense discussions in which I felt irrationally threatened or insulted. Any other parts of me you don't want carried through to our children?

"Just need to find a doctor who thinks this is a medical necessity and is willing to fight for it," Wanda is saying. "To me, this is another form of discrimination."

True enough. I've known many medical professionals who've disparaged my reproductive prospects—X-ray techs who say, "What're *you* worrying about?" when I request a lead shield to protect my precious gonads. I understand Wanda's anger. But couldn't she just wait till they're married? Or does she need to know beforehand? Is her genetic makeup a determinant of her willingness to go through with wedding plans?

"It's just to be informed," she tells me. "It might help us decide if we need to buy a child from China"—she laughs, and her voice chokes for a moment—"or are we going to be okay with having children of our own? Knowing my genetics wouldn't really change anything, other than the fact that it'll give me a little more credibility with my parents." They don't exactly relish the possibility of having grandchildren with SMA.

She still thinks they'll come around, her parents. But she's trying to arm herself with arguments to push them in the right direction. She's also searched libraries for academic work on interabled couples—actual case studies to present to her parents—but so far has come up empty.

It's not just her parents and doctors who have a hard time with Wanda and Kevin's couplehood. When she and Kevin go out on a date, she says, they're frequently subjected to strangers' unwelcome comments. Sounds familiar, I tell her.

"People simply look at us weird sometimes," she says, pausing just short of uttering the word "prejudice." "We are an interracial couple, so racism is something I sort of expected. What angered me the most was the day we went to a coffee shop with Kevin's older brother, who also has SMA, and this well-meaning young girl comes over to our table and says, 'Excuse me, but I'd like to pray for y'all.' And I thought, *Oh fuck! Fuck! Fuck! Is this acceptable?*"

Kevin, says Wanda, blew it off. He was used to this sort of treatment from strangers. Wanda felt otherwise. "My concern at that point was, how is he going to handle that kind of situation if we have kids with us? Do we just avoid going out to eat? I don't want our kids thinking there is something wrong with their dad. I mean, yeah, he's in a wheelchair, but that's different. That's not something to pray over. That's not something for strangers to judge or comment on!"

Wanda finishes by telling me they have another, unrelated hurdle. "He's Catholic," she says. "Since I was married before, we'll have to get a Catholic annulment."

The issue of religion, finally, helps me to universalize much of Wanda and Kevin's interabled experiences. It puts them in context, puts the whole thing in perspective. All couples have their differences, their impediments to clamber over, their tribal expectations to meet or willfully oppose. Interabled couples aren't the only ones. And if these irritations, however maddening and nonsensical, don't drive a wedge between you, they can strengthen you. They can draw you closer together.

Then something else occurs to me. I wonder if coming from different ethnic backgrounds actually makes interability easier. Are two people who come from two different traditions and end up together already looking to break away from the familiar? Certainly M.L. and I faced many discrepancies beyond disability: religion, geography, a taste for debate and discussion versus taking prompt practical action. Yet each of us was looking for something unlike what we'd known growing up. Maybe people like us are predisposed to be open, to learn about and welcome a different set of tastes, needs, habits, goals.

One thing is clear: if Wanda and Kevin are going to go ahead with their plans to marry, they will have to face down a horde of deterrents, not the least of which is her desire for parental approval. Wanda may not be able to change her parents' minds, but she can decide to go her own way regardless. "Most of our stress comes from others' negative reactions," says Kevin, in a subsequent e-mail exchange. "[But] a lot of the stress disintegrates when we're finally able to see each other after a week, two weeks, or even a whole month apart. When I'm with her, all my problems vanish."

He concedes that "some of the stress has also come from the fact that I can't physically do some things that would make our lives easier." I can't help thinking, *Don't we all wish we could do more for our partners?* Call me a romantic, but I believe he and Wanda can emerge from these frustrations.

A year after Wanda's Christmas intervention with her family, the following happens: "I decided not to go back to California this winter," she tells me, "because my parents are not willing to accept Kevin coming with me, and I did not want to spend Christmas without him."

I take her willingness to follow her heart as a good sign. Yet the couple has so many demons to fight still, I can't help feeling left in suspense, wondering if it's really going to work out for them.

RACHELLE AND CHRIS

———•———

THEIR LOVE MAY sound idyllic, but their tale is the stuff of tabloids.

On May 23, 2010, at her bachelorette party a few nights before her wedding was supposed to take place, Rachelle Friedman—an all-American-girl type from suburban North Carolina—was drinking with her best girlfriends when one of them playfully pushed her into the swimming pool, wherein she injured her spine at the C6 cervical nerve and lost the use of her legs.

Rachelle's injury delayed the wedding by nearly a year, but it didn't stop it. Her eventual marriage to her longtime sweetheart, Chris Chapman, garnered so much attention that it became a feature on the *Today* show and in *People* magazine, among other venues.

I'm eager to talk to Rachelle and Chris for several reasons. First, they're a young couple who surmounted their obstacles and effected their dream of matrimony. Second, the couples I've spoken to so far consisted of a disabled male and an able-bodied female; Rachelle and Chris are the other way around. My interest isn't just a matter of gender fairness. A friend of mine once insisted that disabled men have an easier time finding lovers and spouses of the opposite sex than disabled women do, because women are predisposed to be nurturing and caregiving. Then another friend proffered precisely the opposite observation: women, he reasoned, seek a man who is strong and independent and can protect them, thus ruling out most disabled men by virtue of the assumption that they can't provide what women want.

I was eager to prove them both wrong. Even if there's statistical evidence supporting one or the other view—and logically, both can't be true—averages or historical trends don't determine one's fate. I'm all about beating the odds.

Now in their early thirties, Rachelle and Chris live in Knightdale, North Carolina—a leafy suburb of Raleigh with a rapidly growing population, largely thanks to its location within the Research Triangle. I reach Rachelle by phone and can hear her busy household in the background. She sounds calm and confident, but I know it wasn't always so and sometimes still isn't.

The couple's big news: in April 2015—almost exactly a year before our first conversation—they had a baby, Kaylee, thanks to a surrogate. The three were promptly featured again in the media: *Cosmo*, *Inside Edition*, and elsewhere.

"Before my accident, Chris and I were joined-at-the-hip in love and best friends. I don't think we could've gotten any closer," she tells me. "Then the accident happened—and we stayed that way!"

She speaks clearly, but her breathing capacity is somewhat limited. She's regained use of her arms, but her hands have some paralysis; she can't grip or grasp. She also has little or no bladder or bowel control. Still, she has the strength to transfer herself from wheelchair to bed and vice versa, to change her suprapubic catheter—an external tube that attaches to an opening in her lower abdomen to ensure that her bladder empties completely—and to apply her own makeup and style her sunny blond mane. (A common complaint among quadriplegic women: no one can get their look right!)

"I can get myself into bed, get myself undressed and everything—I've even stayed all weekend alone, with no one to help. But it's really tiring, especially after a long day," she wants me to know. "So usually I do what I can, and then Chris kind of helps me with the rest, cheering me along." But she tries to keep her husband's help with her daily needs "to a minimum," she says.

After the wedding but before Kaylee arrived, Rachelle published a harrowing, moving, but ultimately upbeat memoir called *The Promise: A Tragic Accident, a Paralyzed Bride, and the Power of Love, Loyalty, and Friendship.* To say Rachelle isn't shy is putting it mildly. Shortly after Kaylee's birth, the new mom published arty soft-focus boudoir portraits of herself stretched out in bed in her underwear—catheter and all. "I wanted to do something for not only my confidence, but for anyone in my situation who thinks they aren't beautiful because of a flaw," she explained on Facebook. "The paralysis is part of me. The catheter is part of me, but neither is all of me. Confidence will outshine flaws. I'm doing this for those who can't see past a wheelchair. I'm doing it to show that we are capable, sexual beings and we are not to be overlooked."

I take note of her focus on "flaws." It bothers me. I don't consider disability a flaw, just a trait like any other. But I don't say anything.

Clearly, Rachelle sees these revealing photo displays as a form of activism. "I hope it will make people think. People with disabilities still have sexuality. . . . Honestly, I'm tired of [this] being something that we can't talk about as a society," she told the *Huffington Post*, where she frequently blogs. She added in a *People* interview: "I want to put a different face to disability."

Chris, Rachelle's husband, is often photographed beside her—though not in the boudoir portraits—in jeans and a T-shirt, his close-cropped black hair and hint of a beard framing his deep-set eyes and cleft chin. He's a pleasant-looking joe with a shy but gracious smile. I daresay he looks like the eighth-grade science teacher he is (except no glasses or bowtie). "I'm pretty good with the media," he tells me. "Neither of us gets nervous being photographed, but I'm not the best at opening up during interviews. And she's got the social media thing down."

He strikes me as even-tempered and laid-back. No doubt he's devoted to Rachelle. As they near their fifth wedding anniversary, I'm eager to gain a sense of exactly what keeps their passion alive.

"I don't think my disability brought us closer together or made us stronger," Rachelle responds. "But it reaffirmed what we'd thought before. It reaffirmed what we already knew was there."

Fair enough, but it was obviously an adjustment, a learning experience for both of them, right? "You're thrown into a new world," says Chris.

A new world because neither one of them had had any prior experience with disabled people, though now they know quite a few. When I ask how, Chris mentions that Rachelle plays wheelchair rugby—the sport depicted in the 2005 film *Murderball*—on a team with other paraplegic and quadriplegic jocks. "I know all those guys," he says, "and I've learned that people are more able and athletic than I'd thought."

Discovering the true potential and full lives of disabled people is one thing, but it doesn't really answer my query about how they keep their passion going. How did they learn to dig down deep and sustain their abiding love in such profoundly changed circumstances, to nurture that capability within themselves? For an answer to that, I have to bide my time, wait till they're more comfortable with me.

I turn to more practical aspects: How do they manage their daily lives? They're aided most weekdays by Rachelle's mother. "Maybe it's not normal, but she's one of my best friends, and we all get along really well," Rachelle tells me. "I don't know how it works, but it does."

Sounds nice, I consider inwardly, but who really wants mom around all the time, no matter how well you get along? Then again, I reflect, grandparents can be awfully helpful with a new baby. "What exactly does your mom do for you? What's the division of labor?" I ask.

"Well, I do the laundry for everyone," says Rachelle. "Mom cooks, and we both clean. Chris is the one who works full time, so he doesn't do a lot of housework."

Rachelle would like to find a paying job outside the house, but so far she hasn't been able to. "You do all the laundry?" I ask.

I sense that she's pursing her lips in a smile, maybe nodding—but of course that's just my imagination. Her voice becomes so animated, so oxygenated, it has a *You Are There* quality that draws me in. "I do have an accessible kitchen and laundry room," she says.

I draw myself out again, shift perspectives, and ask, "But what about things for you—personal tasks? Is your mom there for that too?"

Rachelle doesn't pause to answer. I get the impression she's been interviewed so often she's ready for anything. Not that her answers are rehearsed or artificial. They're undoubtedly sincere. They seem to issue from her as guilelessly and naturally as a stream flowing between rocks. "Mom helps out with me to try to take as much medical stuff away from Chris, stuff that *has* to be done. Obviously, Chris does do medical stuff for me—and he's done everything!" She takes a breath, emits a small laugh. "But the less he has to do like that, you know, the more normal our relationship is."

I understand what she means, but I can't help feeling she's sugarcoating, deflecting from the gross details of her everyday life. Can't blame her, really. I challenge Chris to explain how they keep the raw work of managing quadriplegia from becoming an obstacle to romance. This may begin to address the passion question.

"I just don't think about it," he answers. A sigh follows, perhaps a shrug. "She doesn't need that much help," he goes on. "I do help her with transfers, dressing, and, rarely, bathroom stuff. But it is what it is. We take care of it and go about our time having fun."

It is what it is. How Zen, or something. "What about with the baby?" I ask, realizing, as I'm mentally directing the question to Rachelle, my own unconscious sexism showing. I can hear Kaylee in the background, perhaps her grandma too, which is what prompted the question. They also have two dogs, who at the moment are quiet.

"At first it was easier than it is now," says Rachelle. "I could hold her. I even got to the point where I could change her diaper!

A lot of things were easier because she wasn't mobile. But now she rolls—I used to be the one to put her to sleep. Me. I would just put her in her crib, use my arm to lift her head, and feed her the bottle. She'd fall asleep, and I'd leave. It was perfect. But now—"

A note of exasperation enters her voice. As Kaylee grew, Rachelle explains, she became more active. She'd fight back. At the time of our conversation, she's in a particularly obstreperous phase. "She just rolls all over the place," Rachelle shares. "It's kind of crazy, and I can't deal with that. Even my husband and my mom have a hard time changing her diaper because she's literally rolling all over the place. So at this point I can't be involved in that part—diaper changing and all that."

"But you can supervise, right?" I say, trying to sound knowledgeable and comforting.

"Yeah."

There's an interruption. I hear a scolding tone followed by what could be the clatter of pots and pans hitting the kitchen floor. "Aw, what'd she do?" says Rachelle, turning away from the phone. "Hold on one sec." The unmistakable sound of a baby crying rings out. Embarrassing for the mother, perhaps, but I smile. It's the telltale sign of a normal, healthy baby so full of life she can't contain herself.

And I realize there are many ordinary distractions to keeping romantic passion alive. Work, children. Perhaps, in this case at least, disability is just one of them.

In her book, Rachelle waxes eloquent about the indomitability of the love she and Chris share and the reasons they decided to wed after her accident:

> We'd always been affectionate, but in the wake of the accident, after a year of being in it together as a team, we'd learned to be so grateful for each other and our love. After we returned home from rehab, Chris got into the habit of hugging me as soon as he walked in the door, a gesture I greatly anticipated each afternoon.

We'd mindlessly done it before, but after the accident we did it with intent. At night, as we lay in bed, he would say, "I love you, sweetheart" and then I would rub his back gently until he started snoring. Each morning, he made my day by saying, "Good morning, beautiful." We never left each other without a kiss and an "I love you" exchange. . . . The year that brought us so much tragedy had also enriched our lives. We never let one day pass without our special moments. We'd become painfully aware of how quickly and drastically life could change. No one knew what the next day would bring, so neither of us wasted time not loving one another fully or taking our love for granted.

Sounds nice, but everyone wasn't so sure. "Chris's parents were concerned," she tells me, the rhythm of her speech slowing, as if she's being careful not to offend them in absentia, "but they're not around us enough to know what we're like. They're not really involved in our lives much."

She doesn't sound angry, telling me about that. She and Chris themselves never had any doubt. "This is hard to explain," she says, "but honestly, there was never a question about whether we would be married."

Her mother was a tad worried early on, Rachelle acknowledges, such as when Rachelle was still in the hospital after her accident. Overhearing us now, her mother pipes in with, "Oh, yeah, I was worried!" They laugh in unison.

Rachelle catches her breath. "I knew Chris wouldn't leave me in the ICU or whatever," she explains, "but my mom wasn't super around him enough then to know that. By the time we did get married, though, everyone was really excited for us."

Their next step, a baby through surrogacy—medically, Rachelle can't sustain a pregnancy—just seemed part of a natural progression. "My mom really wanted me to have my dream of motherhood. She expected she'd have to do a lot, and unfortunately, at times it feels like it's even more than she imagined, because there's more that I thought I'd be able to do and can't."

Hey, it takes a village, I start to mutter. But I don't say it, fearing it'll sound glib or dismissive. With a first baby, I recall, a few stressful moments can make the whole proposition feel impossibly and endlessly arduous. I have memories of repeatedly reassuring M.L. that, no, it won't always be like this. The child will learn to eat without burping up and to walk and talk and go to the potty. She knew it, of course, but sleep deprived and worn ragged as we often were, we were both predisposed to hopelessness and doubt.

Rachelle is confident things will improve. She's faced down plenty of doubt and hopelessness of her own and come out on top. "I had some uncles and aunts and cousins who were like, 'How are you going to be able to take care of a baby?' But again, those people aren't around me, and they don't know what I can and can't do."

Later, I ask Rachelle to describe some of her best moments with Kaylee. She thinks for a beat or two. There are many joys, I'm sure, mixed with fatigue and befuddlement. To pick out one example, especially in the fog of young parenthood, may be asking too much. "At night," Rachelle begins, "one of the things I do is, if she wakes up, Chris'll hand Kaylee to me in bed, and I'll hold her while I'm lying down, and I'll cuddle her. Then he'll bring me the bottle, and I'll put her back to sleep. So he doesn't have to stay awake and feed her. That's something I do. I'll hold her and feed her till she's asleep."

I imagine the halcyon tableau. I've seen Kaylee's picture on Instagram and Facebook; Rachelle posts a lot, an understandably proud mama. She brings her online followers along on her "amazing adventure," wheelchair-based motherhood. I suppose that, in part, has to do with her young age, a generation for whom privacy seems to matter less than it does to geezers like me. But I'd guess too that Rachelle is trying to quash the doubters and naysayers, those who were critical of her marriage, let alone her parenthood.

Rachelle's confidence in their union remains so undiminished, I can't help wondering, What's the secret? What are her tips? "A lot of people think they're in love and someone loves them, and

everything is great," says Rachelle during our next chat. "But if
something goes wrong, it can end the relationship. So it turns out
their love wasn't as strong as they'd thought. . . . Our relationship
proved to be strong. We're just two people who love each other and
can deal with each other's flaws—love each other, flaws and all."

A true romantic—and so young, muses the old man I've become. But she's now thirty, and Chris is thirty-four, so they're
not kids. The word "flaws" gives me pause, though, just as it did
before. This time I ask her to expand on the *flaw* idea. Was she
referring entirely to her disability or to something else? "Does
Chris have flaws?"

He isn't home, so I figure it's a safe question. Yet she hesitates.
Doesn't want to speak ill of her hubby. I want to reassure her
that I'm not looking for dirt, just a better understanding. But the
moment passes.

"You can't necessarily *see* his flaws," she says. "That sounded
so bad. He is amazing, and we fit perfectly. But he has anxiety, I
guess you could say, and I'm the person who calms him down. . . .
Little things can bother him. But I'm super grounded. I don't get
worked up. I tell him, 'It's okay, relax.' I act as his rock."

Trying to picture this, I say something stupid like, "Oh?"

"Honestly, without me, I don't know what he'd do with his
general anxiety—and that's not something you can see, like a
wheelchair."

So she sees her wheelchair as a flaw? If so, that's too bad. But to
me, the conversation is picking up! I like the idea that she doesn't
just take from him but gives something in return too. Or that
she provides for his well-being just as he does for hers. Frankly,
it's often bugged me that people don't see what I do for M.L. In
truth, what they see and think is usually the opposite end of the
spectrum—that my wife is a self-reliant, selfless superwoman who
doesn't ever need or get any help. Yes, she's super, but she's human and not perfect. The point is, I keep this family going as much
as she does, just in different ways. It's more than keeping track of
bills and the social calendar and kids' events and family birthdays

that I contribute, thanks very much. And I'm sure if you asked her, M.L. would say the same.

"It's really important," Rachelle is saying. "A lot of people feel that, with an interabled couple, the able-bodied person is some kind of hero just because he's with you. That's messed up!" Just the other day, she tells me, a man at the mall tapped Chris on the shoulder, shook his hand, and said, "You're my hero." "It doesn't take a hero to be with somebody," Rachelle continues. "I mean, that's basically saying it takes an extraordinary person to deal with someone like me, when really it's just that we're both in love."

Rachelle says it makes her feel as if they're saying she should be "so grateful" and that Chris has all the control in their relationship. "It's not like one of us is forcing the other. We share the power equally," she says. "I'd never leave him, but not because I can't due to my disability or something like that. I'd never leave him because I love him. It's not fair to think otherwise. It's not true, not how it is with us."

When I ask him about this later, Chris says he's insulted by such encounters too, though he rarely makes a fuss. "I just smile and move on," he says. "But I'm with her for *me*. Because I want to be. Not because I feel guilty or am doing her a favor."

I think M.L. could probably say the same, though I doubt she'd smile and move on. Maybe when we were younger and shyer, and this was all new to us, but not anymore. She gets pretty fed up with strangers' clueless comments, and I don't blame her.

Just then, Rachelle wants to correct something, in case I misunderstood. "Don't get me wrong—being with me doesn't make Chris a hero, but he's *my* hero," she says. I picture that thousand-watt, cover-girl smile I've seen online and in magazine pages. "Being with me isn't a heroic act. It doesn't even mean he's a good person. He is, but that's not what it means. He's not inspiring because we've stayed together. Our love—us together—*that's* what should be inspiring. That's what I want to get across. Someone should get inspiration from the fact that we chose love. The fact that we stay together should reflect on us together."

Her outrage is not targeted just at strangers in the shopping mall. Because her story has been so public, she gets many reactions online—not all of them good. She's amassed an arsenal of comebacks. And suddenly I see why she always stresses the depth and honesty of their love. She's defending the fort—a fort fashioned by real, mutual, romantic love, she's saying, not by charity or desperation or obligation or guilt. Or heroics.

Upon reflection, I don't really think she sees her disability as a flaw after all. Rather, it's the perception of a flaw that she's talking about.

Several weeks go by before we connect again. Besides being a busy mom, Rachelle has other media to answer to. A few days after our last talk, she appeared in the *Bump* magazine in a piece called "7 Parenting Lessons from the Paralyzed Bride." She and Chris are also being interviewed for an upcoming TV special on the TLC cable network.

"Ever get mad at each other?" I ask when at last we find a moment. It's just Rachelle this time. I've promised to keep it brief—but the question is crucial. It's hard to get help from or give help to someone you'd rather strangle. What do they do? How do they handle it?

I hear throat clearing, then: "I don't know how to explain it, but we don't get pissed at each other. We literally don't fight. When we bicker, it lasts a short time, and then it's over."

My mouth opens but no words come out. I'm a lifelong, card-carrying member of the skeptics and cynics club, I guess. Finally I say, "But all couples—"

"Sure. I know. There are little things that annoy you when you live with somebody," she allows. "That's part of a normal marriage. For instance, he likes to play his music really loud. So loud it scares the crap out of me every time. I'm like, 'Seriously, stop doing that!' Little things like that, like any normal couple, where you bicker about little things like that, but at the end of the day, you choose love. You choose each other."

Fair enough, but from a disabilities perspective that can get hairy, bickering with someone on whom you rely for nose blowing and ass wiping. I put it differently: "But it's awkward, no, getting help if one of you is in a bad mood?"

She takes a deep breath. She's having none of it. "It's not like I watch what I say because I'm so thankful he's here," she says. "Not like I don't call him out on things that annoy me."

I try to imagine it but can't.

Several weeks go by. I round out our talks by asking Rachelle and Chris, together, about their future plans. "No idea," she says. "We've talked about moving, but we need to stay close to my mom."

"What about that?" I ask. "What happens when your mom can no longer provide the help you need? Have you talked about hiring outside help?"

"We'll have to someday," says Chris. "But we can't afford it right now."

I'm again silently grateful for my family's generous financial support, without which I don't know where I'd be. "Let's talk about something more pleasant," I say. "What do you guys do for fun?"

"We go on vacations together, long weekends," says Rachelle.

"How does that work out?"

"Sure, he has to help more when we're away. Stuff happens. But it's not like every time something goes wrong we freak out. This is our lives now."

Whenever M.L. and I have gone away—I use the past-perfect tense because it's been forever—it's unduly taxing on us both. Without my paid attendant, accustomed commode chair, and other apparatus, even the fanciest resort can feel like nativist camping.

Rachelle acknowledges that Chris usually takes the wheel of their modified van, though she does have a license. Driving, even with hand controls, is "a lot of work," she says. "I have to transfer into a driver's chair and swing my legs around and get situated—it takes me ten minutes! I'm still a little nervous about it. It's unnerving driving around in this huge van too."

I'm surprised she has to transfer out of her wheelchair. Couldn't she remove the driver's seat and access all controls from her wheelchair, as many other crips do? (Not me, because I don't have the necessary strength or stability to drive, even with hand controls.) I ask if there isn't some way to make driving easier for her.

"I'm definitely working on it," she says. "I want to be completely independent."

"Of course," I say, to sound sympathetic (but I fear it comes off avuncular or even condescending). I wonder if that's the linchpin of their relationship—her all-encompassing desire for self-reliance. Is that what motivates her and ultimately, in a way, keeps their love alive? I ask if that's the one thing she would change if she could, her level of independence.

"You mean besides finding a cure?" She laughs, then comes back with a long response I didn't expect. "Obviously that's something I want, but I don't consider walking to be the biggest deal. People see my situation and say, 'Oh, we want you to walk again.' But that's literally the least of the things I'd want back. If I just had finger function again. . . ." She manages to do many things with her hands, but the paralysis there impedes her interactions with Kaylee. And that bothers her most of all. "People say, 'If she's in a wheelchair, how is she going to be a mom?' But they don't even know what they're talking about," she continues. "It's not the wheelchair. It's the hand functions. Not being able to grip anything. If I'm feeding her and all of a sudden she does this weird movement, it knocks the food right out of my hands because I'm barely able to grip it."

Finger function would give her greater autonomy, she says. "Really, whatever would allow me to do more and take it off everybody else would make everything so much better, and in my opinion that would be finger function."

Her words echo the wishes of many, no doubt. But I'm hearing something more. It's not just a desire for independence—which, let's face it, can be improved with better access, technology, financial resources, and barrier-removal as much as with medical advances. Rachelle also yearns to be heard and not judged. She doesn't want others to define her.

As for my initial question about what keeps their passion alive, I'm beginning to wonder if I've been obtuse. Perhaps, as she says, it does ultimately come down to nothing more than choosing to stay together. Or, as she would say, choosing love.

PART II

THE LONG AND WINDING ROAD

ALISHA AND JARED

———◆———

THE HISTORY OF PEOPLE with disabilities is inarguably tied up with war. According to the Disability Social History Project, the earliest known adaptive devices were prosthetic limbs made for warriors: the first record of such a tool can be found in India's Rig Veda, an ancient collection of Vedic Sanskrit hymns dated between 3500 and 1800 BCE that tells of one Queen Vishpala, whose leg was severed in battle and replaced with an artificial appendage so she could return to combat. Eons later, in 218 BCE, at the start of the Second Punic War, a Roman general's arm was similarly severed, yet he resumed fighting thanks to an iron hand. (Later, alas, he was turned away from the priesthood because his deformity prevented him from performing the duties of the office.)

All this runs through my head as I think about the wounded warriors of modern times. I dislike the connection between violence and disability rights, but I know it's real. I know that the first federal vocational rehabilitation program was only established in the wake of World War I and that the first Employ the Physically Handicapped Week was inaugurated by President Harry Truman in response to the wave of disabled vets returning from World War II.

It's estimated that more than a million (and counting) wounded warriors have returned from the twenty-first century's wars in Afghanistan and Iraq. (The Department of Veterans Affairs stopped releasing figures some time ago.) In earlier conflicts, many of these survivors would've died from their wounds. Plus, we've begun to recognize traumatic brain injuries and psychological disabilities such as PTSD, which impinge on one's functioning as surely as amputations and other, gorier physical damage.

Many of these injured souls come home to young girlfriends or boyfriends or spouses, and together they struggle to remake their lives. Accommodating the impaired multitudes remains an underreported challenge for our country. All told, the divorce rate among profoundly altered heroes is high. The stresses prove too great.

Yet somehow, many such couples *do* stay together. They manage to adjust, adapt, and re-form their relationships around their new reality. With deference, humility, and trepidation, I seek out one such successful couple.

In an online newspaper I read about Alisha and Jared. (I'm withholding their last names at their request.) He's a maintenance mechanic, Jared says when I reach them by online video conference, currently employed at a college campus in the Pacific Northwest; she's the owner of a home-based business called Fantasy Clay Flowers, which makes handmade decorative creations sold through Etsy, Amazon, and other online retailers. They're in their early thirties and have a six-year-old son and a daughter on the way.

Jared is an Iraq War veteran. A big, soft-spoken man, he served eight years as an active duty infantryman. Deployed with the Joint Base Lewis-McChord Stryker Brigade in 2004, he served as squad leader in Mosul and rose to the level of platoon sergeant. His final nine months of active duty were spent as a special duty chaplain's assistant, aiding in military funerals. In all, he says, he helped bury thirty-four colleagues.

Alisha picks up the story.

"When Jared returned from his deployment, I noticed right away that he was different," she says. Her voice is cheery and upbeat. Less than five feet tall and seven months pregnant when we first chat, she seems not one bit weighed down by it. Then she pauses, shakes her blond hair. "He was already struggling."

This was nine years ago. The struggles she refers to took many forms. Sometimes he couldn't get up in the morning, she tells me, and he had difficulty finding and keeping employment. Asked what was wrong, he'd refuse to answer.

"He put up a tough fight about letting anyone, even me, help him," says Alisha, her green eyes growing moist. What followed was something akin to the stages of grief. "There was denial, anger, frustration, and resentment. On both of our parts," she says. "We mourned the life that we thought we would have, the life we deserved."

Jared struggled for nearly four years before doctors came up with a firm diagnosis.

"Eventually, I was diagnosed with chronic and severe post-traumatic stress disorder with anxiety and depression," says Jared, his voice strong and clear now, gaining momentum. At nearly a foot taller than Alisha, with short dirty-blond hair, penetrating cobalt-blue eyes, and the sort of big bushy beard many young men sport these days, he exudes a calm charisma that makes me want to know more about him. "This condition hasn't changed from the day I was diagnosed to today," he says.

Psychological disabilities like he's describing aren't ever cured, but you can develop strategies for coping with them. The first step, of course, is diagnosis—naming what's going on, on the inside. That was a big step.

"We were faced with a serious, complex set of problems that we never asked for and didn't expect to have to deal with," recalls Alisha. "We were inexperienced in the arena of mental health issues, and we had to grow up fast and learn how to cope."

Military deployment and disability have that in common, I think as she's talking. Both make you grow up fast.

Jared was just seventeen when he signed up with the US Army. He left for basic training less than a week after graduating from high school, at eighteen. About three years later, while stationed at Fort Lewis (now part of Joint Base Lewis-McChord), outside Tacoma, Washington, he met Alisha. She was working at a local store. Six months later they married at the courthouse, with her grandparents as witnesses. He was twenty-two and she, twenty-one. Less than three months after that he was deployed to Iraq.

"We were attracted to each other for different reasons," Alisha reflects, conjuring what's plainly a sweet memory. Her smiling face brightens. "I was attracted to Jared's intelligence; his silly, goofy nature; and his people skills. He was charming and sweet, friendly and smart and outgoing." These traits haven't changed, she assures me, but in the intervening years their relationship has evolved. Putting her current feelings about him into words is, she says, "like trying to describe why you appreciate your right arm. You don't really think about it; it's just something you count on that's always there."

She swallows. They glance at each other.

"He's still smart and funny, and I appreciate the hard work he puts into making our life together the best it can be. It also turns out he's a good father, which is a bonus."

When it's Jared's turn, he says, "I was attracted to myself because I am incredibly good-looking," evidencing that silly, goofy nature Alisha referred to. "So good-looking I almost became a male model, but I wasn't smart enough."

We all laugh. But of course, he can't get off the hook that easily.

"I was attracted to Alisha from the very first time I spoke to her," he says then, turning his eyes from hers to some invisible point on the ground. After a moment, I prompt him for elaboration. "She was caring and sweet and compassionate, a family-oriented, mentally tough woman. These things are still true today. I was lucky enough to marry my best friend."

Since Jared's return from Iraq, Alisha has been his caregiver. That's an official term, bestowed by the US government. In 2010, Congress passed the Caregivers and Veterans Omnibus Health Services Act, which directed the Veterans Administration to provide additional counseling and financial assistance to those injured in the line of duty since the terrorist attacks of 9/11. This support goes beyond the usual counseling, rehabilitation, and retraining available for all disabled veterans. It also enables post-9/11 vets to apply for a financial stipend for designated caregivers.

As often as not, those caregivers are family members. Like Alisha. Alisha began receiving her caregiving stipend—something over $1,000 a month—in 2012. "For about two years, I was Jared's Certified Caregiver through [the VA] program," she says. As such, her job was to help Jared cope: To help him feel safe. To provide consistency and calm control. To manage his meds. To figure out what he needed to do or have done to feel better. To take full responsibility for financial matters. To provide moral support when he's so depressed he can't get out of bed. To aid with stress and anger management. One example: Alisha arranged to have trees removed from their front yard to give Jared a clear view of anyone approaching their house.

"I've been the one to help him and care for him when he is having serious or minor issues related to his diagnosis," she says. Day to day, that care may include everything from grocery shopping and meal preparation to "making sure he eats," she says, "scheduling appointments and accompanying him, [and] making sure he didn't/doesn't injure himself when he's having night terrors or sleepwalking."

She cuts his hair, which he likes to keep close-cropped.

"He can't handle a stranger with scissors or sharp instruments near his head and neck. Even a trained barber."

Alisha acknowledges having some previous experience with people with disabilities, but nothing helpful, nothing like having a husband with PTSD. "My experiences with disabled people were varied," she says. There were a couple of friends from school who were "differently abled," she says. "I also have two cousins who were born with serious birth defects. . . . They were just my little cousins, who I played with and loved. Their disabilities were kind of an afterthought."

So, she says, she taught herself "what to do and how to help when he needs it." Even so, qualifying for the VA caregiver stipend wasn't a sure thing. She had to escort Jared to countless doctor visits in order to prove that he needed the program.

"We've been to many, many medical appointments," she relates, emitting an undisguised groan. "Early on, just getting seen and being diagnosed so that we could begin to get help was a huge challenge in itself!"

Private long-term-care insurance only kicks in if you're unable to perform at least two "activities of daily living" (for example, bathing, dressing, toileting). With the VA caregiver program, however, all that's required is the need for assistance with one such activity. That assistance doesn't have to be physical in nature. It can include supervision or protection from self-harm due to battle-related cognitive or psychiatric impairment. The dollar amount is based on the going rate among commercial home-health-care agencies in the area. One 2016 survey shows the program has grown by more than four hundred recipients a month, despite some dropping off the roster because they no longer qualify.

"Since his diagnosis is psychological in nature, it's been an ongoing challenge," Alisha tells me. "I am constantly trying to hit a moving target."

But with the VA stipend, she could devote nearly all her time to Jared and their son. They were managing. "We had to make huge adjustments to our everyday lives," she says, including giving up most social activities. Nevertheless, in time, they achieved a certain rhythm. Until everything changed again.

The VA is required to monitor each recipient to determine how they're doing and whether the funds are being well spent, Alisha explains. Home visits are not uncommon. Those who don't pass muster must undergo "corrective steps," such as additional training or, in some cases, a termination of benefits.

In December 2015, after two and a half years in the program, Alisha and Jared were terminated from the caregiver stipend without explanation. They still have no idea why.

According to press reports, they are far from alone. It's estimated that seven thousand vets who were once enrolled in the caregiver program have been terminated. The VA claims that a third of them no longer need the assistance or no longer meet the medical criteria. As for the other two-thirds, however, no explanation is given.

Alisha and Jared understand that the stipend was never intended to be permanent, even though most disabilities sustained in battle *are* permanent. They point me to a 2014 study from the Government Accountability Office, which indicates that the program was severely underfunded from day one. Original projections anticipated that only a total of four thousand vets would qualify. In fact, nearly four times that many had enrolled by 2014. Now the roster has swelled to more than twenty-five thousand recipients and counting.

The good news is, Alisha and Jared are not without recourse— some members of Congress are pushing for an expansion of the program. The couple also has a strong advocate in a nonprofit lobbying group called Disabled American Veterans. DAV insists that family members who provide personal-care assistance for wounded warriors are carrying out the nation's responsibility to its veterans and, therefore, plainly deserve to be compensated.

In 2016, the VA caregiver program was budgeted at $555 million, but supporters say that's a bargain compared to the cost of institutional care.

"I told the VA over and over. I don't know if they're not writing it down, if they don't think it's [a valid] issue or what the deal is, but [our situation] has never been addressed," Alisha told the Tacoma *News Tribune* in January 2016.

A year later, they're still appealing the decision.

Yet somehow, Alisha and Jared sound optimistic. They're not whiners. In our next conversation, I ask her how exactly they've managed.

"In the end, we had to learn to trust each other, how to rely on each other, and how to be dependable and stable for each other. It was a long and difficult process," she shares. She estimates it took three or four years for them to "pull together and move on." Jared's sense of humor helped, she adds, though it's clear to me he's not particularly comfortable talking about these serious matters. I'm basically a stranger to them and not above suspicion. "Nothing was more important than making sure that Jared stayed as safe and well as he could be, and that we stayed together and learned together to make our lives all that we wanted them to be," she says.

I think back to what Jared said earlier and realize how right he is—Alisha *is* family-oriented and mentally tough. "You said before that you had to adjust to things not turning out as you had expected or wanted," I say. "So I imagine you had to make adjustments to the way you interact with each other, the roles each of you play to make your couplehood work. Can you explain how you've re-formed your relationship around your new reality?"

"Sure," she says quickly. But a long pause follows. She's gathering her thoughts, picking her words as carefully as you'd choose vegetables at the market—squeezing and weighing for maximum effect. "This question is extremely complex," she begins.

One part of her answer is suddenly self-evident. In responding to my questions, it's clear she's the one in charge of making sense of what they've endured. She seems to be the couple's chief conduit to the outside world, the spokesperson empowered to articulate the messy, deeply personal, and highly emotional stuff.

It's not that Jared isn't introspective, exactly. He just doesn't like airing his personal issues for public consumption. But he's willing. He understands the need for his story—for their story—to see the light of day, where it might help other couples, especially other vet couples.

"As for the roles we play," says Alisha with a sigh, "Jared calls me Captain, I call him Sergeant. He looks to me for leadership and trusts me to stay calm and clear-headed when he needs help. I rely on him to keep working hard and pushing towards wellness, and to trust me enough to express to me if he needs help."

I learn they've received only scant assistance from their families since Jared's return from Iraq. Their relatives don't disapprove of their marriage per se; they just don't understand what PTSD is and what Alisha and Jared have been going through—or why they have stayed together.

"My family was not exactly kind," she says with a curt chuckle. "There was a scattered, inconsistent effort to understand what was going on and what had changed. But overall, most of my family and extended family were disdainful and standoffish."

Aloud, I wonder why.

"Honestly, I don't really care what the rest of my family thinks anyway," she says. "It's my life. I don't live it for their approval."

Jared concurs. "I don't really care what my family thinks either. But they love Alisha."

Inwardly, I muse that there's nothing like parental disapproval to cement a romantic commitment. For Alisha and Jared, their devotion to each other almost seems to have become stronger as a result of their having to go it alone—although they weren't quite alone.

"The people closest to me, my grandparents, were loving and accepting and supportive," Alisha says then. "They loved Jared before his disability and they loved him after—until the day they passed away. Our union was always supported by them."

✦　✦　✦

Later, I ask why they think some couples stay together after a disabling accident while others fail. What advantages do lasting couples like them have that others lack? To my surprise, I've tapped a rich vein of introspection and wisdom.

"It's very difficult for both people when one half of a couple becomes disabled," says Alisha. "Everything changes, often without warning."

She goes on to express how hard it can be watching a newly disabled partner struggle—not just because of love but because of empathy. You try to understand what they're going through physically and psychologically. You want to help but don't know how. This can lead to a kind of desperation, she says.

"You want to make everything better for them, but you can't. You start out feeling helpless and hopeless, uncertain of what you can do and if your partner even wants your help!"

Jared joins in. "For the disabled partner, it can be hard to accept or reconcile yourself to your disability," he says.

His tone may be soft, but it's sure. Perhaps a discussion they've had before, I'm thinking. Possibly in therapy, given what comes next.

"You might feel like a burden. You may be grieving for the life you had before your disability. You may be feeling unworthy of your partner. You might be doubting whether or not your partner even wants to stay, or wondering if they are staying out of pity or duty."

I have to admit, even a longtime cripple like me has had those kinds of self-doubts. But I don't admit it just then, not aloud. Instead, I ask what advice they'd give other couples, given all these tumultuous feelings and recriminations. They know a few other disabled vets, though none with PTSD, they tell me. Alisha adds that they rarely see them or anyone else socially.

"Still," I prompt, "what tips would you offer those who are struggling to survive?"

"If I had to guess why some couples stick together while others don't," says Alisha, "my guess would be communication. It can be hard to express to your disabled partner your stresses and frustrations. You don't want to make them feel guilty, even if you yourself feel as though you are being taken advantage of, or that you want to rage against the unfairness of it all."

I know all about raging at the unfairness. M.L. and I both do it at times, though we try to let the other know it's nothing personal, just baying at the moon. (That's how a therapist put it to us once, ages ago. "Ask each other, is that a request or are you just howling?" Good advice we still try to follow.)

"But how do you learn to communicate in that healthy way?" I ask.

"For the disabled partner, it can be hard to just work through all of the emotions and traumas of your disability," says Jared. "It's hard to work it out within your own mind, let alone to express it in words to your partner." Insecurity, anger, frustration, guilt—they all conspire against open communication, he says. "It's not easy to say you feel like a burden . . ."

He trails off, but Alisha picks up the loose end. They're in sync. And this, I realize, is one way they help each other. It's an example of how they work together, an indication of the power of their partnership. The power of their pledge to remain partners. Making that pledge, I see now—making it in private, when you really mean it, as opposed to at a marriage ceremony where there are witnesses and expectations and pressures—can create a kind of self-fulfilling prophecy.

"For Jared and me, a little bit of reassurance that we were going to stay together went a long way," she is saying. "Once we had it established that we were going to go on together, we started working as a team. But before the communication was reestablished under these new circumstances, everything was difficult. When you don't communicate with your partner, and you lack an emotional investment and trust, life can be miserable. But once you get back to that foundation of communication and emotional trust, things work out."

Her advice, then, for other couples who are struggling: *stay connected*. Emotionally, physically, and mentally.

"But how do you get there?" I query, pushing my luck.

Alisha answers slowly but emphatically, glancing at Jared for confirmation. "Talk to each other. Listen. Communicate in any way that you are safely able to. If it's hard to talk to your partner, write them a note, write an e-mail, text. Just get your thoughts and feelings out and don't let them bottle up. When things bottle up, resentments build, trust is damaged, and communication suffers."

Easy to say, I think to myself, hating myself for the thought.

Perhaps sensing my skepticism, she adds, "Also, know what your boundaries are and let your partner know. Any relationship takes a lot of dedication and hard work from both parties. If you are both in it for the long distance, make sure that you both know it."

Maybe such dedication comes down to deeds more than words, it occurs to me. Private pledges of allegiance help, to be sure, but there's nothing like actually being there for each other and helping each other through the worst times and appreciating the best times together.

The sun is setting on this winter afternoon, but I'm not quite done yet. "If you could change one thing about your situation, what would it be?" I ask.

"Well, we wouldn't mind being filthy rich, retired, and living on a beautiful beach somewhere." That's Jared, of course. The joker.

But really, I start to say—more money? More help? More privacy from each other? I don't get to articulate any of those things, because Alisha jumps in.

"Overall," she says, "if we had the ability to change anything, it would be the general perception of what PTSD is, what it means to the people who suffer with it, and the importance of taking care of our veterans and their caregivers."

It strikes me how few people answer this question with "to be cured," or even "to have never become disabled in the first place." It's as if their disability experiences have become part of who they are now. Making life easier is always the wish, but not so much through eliminating the diagnosis as shoring up the support systems. I think that's how I'd answer my own question too.

"It's not an easy road to travel," Alisha says, "and veterans need and deserve all the help they can get."

Plainly, Jared's invisible yet profound disability has become an accepted though not welcome part of his family's life. Coping with it has forced him and his wife to communicate with each other more openly and honestly than ever before, it seems, leading them to effectively reaffirm their vows to each other each day. Or am I misunderstanding? Jumping to a self-serving conclusion?

I end with a question to which I believe I already know the answer. But I'm at least partly wrong. "Would you say the disability helps bring you closer as a couple, or is it an obstacle in your relationship—or neither?"

"Neither," says Jared. "It is what it is."

He's having none of the growing-stronger-through-adversity hooey, which my question implied. Perhaps he's too practical-minded for that. That's me, pushing my luck again—hoping for a romantic conclusion.

Then Alisha says, "I would say it's been a mix. In the beginning, I had to fight the urge to run away screaming into the night. But that's not who I am. I don't run away from difficulties. The idea of doing so offends my personal sense of honor. If I had left, I would've been abandoning a man I love while he was in danger, in pain, and in need of help. And over time, I've realized that I made the right decision. It was hard to stay and work through everything, but it was the right choice. We are stronger as a couple. We work well together, understand each other, and love each other."

I smile. I've gotten my happy ending after all.

(Author's note: In May 2017, the VA announced it would temporarily stop kicking veterans' family members out of the caregiver program until a thorough review could be completed.)

ALICE AND BILL

———◆———

ALICE LAWSON, a thirty-five-year-old mother and former pastry chef in Hawaii, has Ehlers-Danlos syndrome. Which I'd never heard of. Which defies easy understanding. Which, over the years, has utterly upended her life. Even learning about it left me feeling emotionally bushwhacked.

Simply put, EDS is a congenital collagen deficiency. Before meeting the Lawsons (whose names have been changed, per their request)—a bright, articulate, self-aware, middle-class couple and their beguiling eight-year-old daughter, Hannah—I only knew of collagen as an ingredient in complexion boosters and from ads for plastic surgeons (of which there are scads in LA). But collagen is serious business.

Here's the sciencey explanation, as best I understand it (feel free to skip the next few paragraphs): Collagen is a protein—the most common protein in our bodies, making up a quarter to a third of our overall protein content—that's essential to the connective tissue that holds all our body parts together, inside and out. EDS destroys that connective tissue, which binds and shapes skin, joints, and blood vessels. An inherited condition—actually a group of at least six different pathologies, according to current medical thinking—EDS can cause rubbery but readily broken skin, dangerously over-flexible joints, easily ruptured intestines, and a host of secondary ailments. Symptoms can appear at any time but become worse—and more obvious—with age. There is no cure.

The good news is that it occurs in only one of every five thousand people—and for the most serious forms, it's more like one in every forty thousand. In comparison, remember that spinal muscular atrophy—my particular neuromuscular delight—is estimated to appear once in every six thousand live births. (But who's counting?)

I don't like harping on medical details. My interest is in people, not diagnoses. But if reading this description makes you look at your own skin with a nervous, quizzical gaze, take heart. Though it's usually first diagnosed from obvious symptoms, there is a genetic test for most varieties of EDS. But if you don't have the symptoms and your forebears didn't either, you probably don't have it.

Alice's specific type, type III, however, is not among the testable forms; the exact genetic marker hasn't been identified yet. Her diagnosis was based on her medical history and a physical exam.

For Alice, the symptoms first revealed themselves strangely and out of the blue, defying easy diagnosis. She had an assortment of related but separate medical problems—or "comorbidities," as she terms them—such as migraines and a painful tightness of the jaw, known as temporomandibular joint disorder, or TMJD, which can trigger terrible headaches and make it hard to eat.

"I knew I had migraines," she recalls, "and had an erroneous fibromyalgia diagnosis. But we had no idea the full extent of what was going on."

Back in 2005, when she was a twenty-four-year-old apprentice pastry chef at an upscale restaurant in downtown Manhattan—she'd moved from a small town in Texas to attend the Culinary Institute of America in Hyde Park, about two hours north of New York City—she was still mostly in the dark about her disability. "Her condition was present but not yet disabling," says Bill, her husband for the past nine years.

Bill was a waiter at the same restaurant, studying to become a financial advisor. He's three years older than she is. Twenty-seven when they met, he was handsome and serious and impressively practical-minded, she recalls. Two years later they married.

"A week before the wedding, I was hospitalized for what we now know was a postural orthostatic tachycardia syncope episode," she says. I had to look it up. POTS is a fairly newly defined disorder—first named in 1993 by a neurological team at the Mayo Clinic—in which the heart races when you stand or sit up, sometimes causing partial or complete loss of consciousness (syncope). POTS is still not well understood. A doctor initially diagnosed Alice with "severe migraine and dehydration," which proved a useless generic assessment. "My migraines became serious enough I had to stop working as a pastry chef," she says. "I took a less stressful office job."

I ask her to clarify whether she quit the pastry job before or after their wedding, but she can't answer. Her disability and the meds she's on now mess with her brain. She giggles, apologizes.

"I'm horrible with dates," she says, "due to the brain fog and cognitive stuff that comes and goes. You probably need to check with Bill for exact dates."

Doesn't matter, that particular detail. Nevertheless, I note that it's my first example of how their marriage works, how they work together to cut a path through the medical miasma.

In time, Alice's New York headache specialist suggested she move out of the city. The constantly changing barometric pressure there seemed to trigger her migraines. She needed more stable weather. So the newly married couple chose Hawaii, settling on the north shore of Oahu, where she hoped to find work in a restaurant or resort hotel. "We moved here with a couple of duffel bags and a few job leads. We knew absolutely no one," she says.

Alice soon discovered she was pregnant. The joyous revelation came with unforeseen medical consequences. Her pregnancy soon became scary.

"I flared hard soon after I became pregnant," she tells me.

That means what she now knows to be her EDS started acting up. EDS symptoms tend to wax and wane, she tells me. "Flares" are what she calls the times when her symptoms are at their most severe. There's not much anyone can do about them. Typically, treatments include ibuprofen and other anti-inflammatories. A rheumatologist may recommend physical therapy to relieve pain and ease mobility. Nonetheless, over time the condition tends to get worse as collagen degrades.

"I was in preterm labor for the majority of the pregnancy and was bed-rested," she says. "I had hyperemesis"—translation: excessive vomiting—"to the point of extreme dehydration, and am allergic or nonresponsive to all the antiemetics on the market. I basically threw up constantly for seven or eight months."

I make a sympathetic sound that I'm certain is inadequate. She goes on with practiced attention to detail.

"Prolactin, a hormone that's released during pregnancy, contributes to tissue laxity, so I had a large increase in subluxations, muscle strain, spasms, and pain," she says, sending me back to the online medical dictionary. (Subluxation is a partial dislocation of the bones in a joint.)

But Hannah arrived unscathed, a healthy baby who is now a healthy eight-year-old girl. Shortly thereafter, Alice received her EDS diagnosis. (It turns out that her POTS is actually a separate spin-off disorder.) "Apparently I was born with EDS," she says now. Thinking back, she realizes she "never felt 'normal' [as a kid]. I spent a lot of time reading instead of playing sports, cooking indoors instead of being outside in the Texas heat. I was compensating without knowing it."

When younger, she could effectively fool others and herself; she could pass for able-bodied. Which was fortuitous both professionally and personally. As a young New York chef, she shares with me, she had a normal sexually active social life—before falling in love with Bill.

✦   ✦   ✦

Today, armed with knowledge about her diagnosis, Alice does her best to keep up with household and parenting responsibilities. But sometimes they feel inordinately onerous, given her constant setbacks. "Depending on how bad I'm flaring, I can go from near abled-bodied to completely bedridden to stuck in the hospital for weeks at a time," she explains. At the time of our conversation, she's in the midst of a bad flare. She's mostly stuck in bed with a peripherally inserted central catheter, or PICC, in a vein in her arm to provide prolonged intravenous treatments (including simple saline, for hydration) and make blood draws easier. Her pain is managed with marijuana and intermittent brain-fogging opioids, she complains. Needless to say, she's bored to death. Which is good for me, because it gives her plenty of time to ponder and talk. That may sound selfish, but she's actually glad about it too.

"I could write *volumes*," she tells me. "I'm really delighted you're doing this. . . . I hope this helps other families."

I'm again struck by her commonsense tone. She doesn't sound as if she's complaining or feeling sorry for herself; she's just excruciatingly aware of what's going on within her . . . and its effects on her family.

"I wish my daughter had a mom who could start a Girl Scout troop and take her camping and to the mall. I wish we had a firm diagnosis of exactly which comorbidities the EDS has stirred up. Having that up in the air makes for some scary times! I wish I could find a part-time virtual job I could do without risking losing my SSDI benefits, so I could help contribute financially."

SSDI refers to Social Security Disability Insurance. It essentially draws on your Social Security account if you're not retired but are unable to work because of a disability. If you are able to work, even a little, chances are you'll lose benefits.

"I feel like a drain a lot of times," Alice tells me. "I wish my husband's life was easier too."

"Your husband's life?" I prompt. Bill is not present at the moment.

"He does the grocery shopping. Walks the dog. Cleans the house. Drives me to appointments. Makes breakfast and lunch for our daughter. He comes home on bad days to check on me, to make sure I eat and I'm comfortable. We keep in contact by phone multiple times a day. I never know how I'm going to feel, and sometimes [things change] hour by hour. So he has no certainty in his life."

Of course, neither does she, I point out. A ponderous, mournful silence follows. I'm thinking, *One person's disability becomes the family's disability.* This particular family does not use hired help on a regular basis, only occasional nurses as needed. They cope in a somewhat ad hoc manner.

"We rely on friends and neighbors for playdates and to pick up and/or drop off our daughter on days I can't drive," she is saying.

Bill is now a certified financial planner and advisor with a retail practice outside Honolulu. His full roster of clients means an ever-busy work schedule. I didn't know Bill before our interview, but I've interviewed many financial advisors throughout my journalism career. I can imagine his workload, his mentality. He's constantly adjusting his schedule to respond to client demands, hold their hands when their portfolios sag, encourage them to adhere to a budget, and pick up the slack when something goes awry at home. Most advisors, I've found, aren't the greedy, self-centered bastards you might imagine from TV. They genuinely want to help people. In fact, they're certified to put others' interests ahead of their own, as part of their fiduciary obligations. Putting Alice and Hannah's interests first, before his own, may be second nature to him. But easy? I doubt it.

In a subsequent e-mail exchange, I get a chance to ask him how he copes. "It depends on the day," he writes. "There have been periods when Alice's capabilities improved and periods of decline."

I ask him to elaborate. His answer sounds a bit too diplomatic to me. Maybe it's his dispassionate professional advisor ethos kicking in.

"She couldn't drive from 2009 to 2012," he says. "Since then she has driven on good days, and there have even been a few days where she could swim or snorkel."

The unpredictability must drive them crazy! But I don't say that. I'm waiting to hear them say it.

"I've had some very scary days, especially pre-diagnosis," Alice adds when we chat later. "Depending on where I am in my flare cycle, Bill either has a lot more work at home or an easier time. Mostly it's more work. Mentally and emotionally, I've improved a lot, but physically I'm a wreck. Bill's abilities as a caregiver have increased exponentially, and I think it makes him a better father."

It makes him a better father? The perks of disability? I put it to him.

"I have seen some of my abilities improve, such as organization, crisis management, patience, leadership skills, cleaning skills," he says, somewhat deflecting. "In other ways I am more reserved, less likely to take chances and less optimistic. There are times when I am in better shape than when we met, and times when I get super lazy."

Alice laughs, but she's having none of it. "My disability has helped him gain empathy." Pause. She catches her breath. "At times, after surgery or [during] bad flares, Bill has helped me with toileting, getting dressed, bathing." It almost seems a painful confession, to my ears—embarrassing to admit to needing bathroom assistance. "I try my best to handle the grody stuff myself."

Something beyond the toilet zone, perhaps? "Such as?" I ask.

"I schedule dressing changes with the home-care nurse for when he's at work," she says, referring to the dressing around her PICC or surgical incisions. "I try to run my fluids when he's not around," she goes on, referring to the carefully measured hydration through that PICC. "It's hard to live with a partner who's turned your bedroom into a hospital room, and he hates gore and hospitals!"

She doesn't want to turn her husband into a nurse either. Can't blame her. I recall M.L.'s reaction a few years ago, after I received my permanent tracheostomy, when she first saw the raw pink hole in my throat. "It looks like a gunshot wound," she said, almost fainting. "I am definitely *not* a nurse!"

Since then, though, M.L. has learned to do many minor medical-ish tasks for me, such as changing my colostomy pouch every week and even occasionally changing the mini-tracheotomy I now sport in that neck hole, when it accidentally pops out. Still makes her nervous, this stuff, but neither of us liked waiting for home nurses or doctor appointments for what are really basic maintenance tasks. There's a terrific sense of pride, of autonomy and privacy, that comes from handling your own needs. When it comes to bloody output, which I still have from my disconnected rectum—believe it or not—she sometimes says, "It's no worse than a bad heavy-flow period." I'll take her word for it.

Still, M.L. hates to be praised for her medical skills, insisting they are out of her comfort zone. "I have no stomach for blood or wounds," she protests. "I'm just a mom, and we get used to disgusting stuff."

Her efficiency with these unpleasant but necessary aspects of my well-being can suffuse me with a warm, oozy mixture of gratitude and insecurity. The weekly colostomy-pouch change, for instance, is a specialized technique involving a spray-on skin-protection barrier, adhesives, and a varying degree of poopy cleanup. Most people with a colostomy do it themselves, but it's another thing to do it for your spouse. We've never trusted my attendant to do it, no matter how good the attendant du jour. As many times as M.L.'s explained the process to me, or to attendants, I doubt I could adequately oversee or instruct someone else to do it. I can't actually see the intestinal stoma area very well anyway—it's in my lower abdomen—without a mirror. If I ever had to fend for myself completely, I think I'd hire a home colostomy nurse to come in weekly to do it. Though that person probably wouldn't do it as well as M.L.

So I think I understand what Alice means about the grody stuff. She wants to spare Bill, but she also wants to spare herself the embarrassment and feelings of powerlessness over her own body.

✦ ✦ ✦

I wonder if anything in Alice's and Bill's backgrounds prepared them for this life, a hidden source of strength, perhaps, such as a disabled sibling or an impervious single parent. I start with Alice. If EDS is an inherited disorder, surely some of her relatives have it too, yes?

"None of my family members have even bothered with EDS testing," she says, "even though we know certain family members *are* badly affected. There's a lot of denial." When Alice told them of her official diagnosis, she continues, her parents scarcely reacted. "Honestly, they were more shocked that I'd married a Jew and converted. We are not close."

Bill reports nothing especially relevant in his background. "None of my close friends growing up or family was disabled." When his family met Alice, they were "happy and reassured," he says. Reassured? I ask. Well, he *was* twenty-seven. They'd thought it was about time. "I had dated regularly, but no one who was serious or long term," he explains.

It helped, perhaps, that at that point Alice's EDS wasn't diagnosed or visible yet. There was no reason for the in-laws to be concerned.

It's a complicated medical history Alice has shared with me. The enlightenment I'm gaining is that not all disabilities fit into a neat classification, such as "wheelchair user." Sometimes Alice's disability isn't so bad, but the uncertainty may almost be the worst part of her condition. I want to know more about the effects of her EDS on her marriage. In our next conversation, I hear a revelation that may shed a bright spotlight on the matrimonial mystery.

"The EDS has ruined my reproductive and digestive systems," she confides. "We're still sexually active, but I can't sleep comfortably next to Bill anymore. So there are challenges at times for intimacy."

Aha! Maybe that's all it comes down to—sex! Certainly the progression of my disability has affected M.L.'s and my sex life, but then again so has aging. Admittedly, the first setback occurred when I stopped being able to caress her with my hands as I had once been able to do, a decline in motor function that is part of the natural progression of my SMA. Then came M.L.'s menopause, during which she experienced a decrease in her libido. But it was after my colostomy-pouch surgery eight years ago (and its dangerous aftermath—near-fatal septicemia, a series of short-term comas, multiple pneumonias, intermittent blood clots, six months of a nasal-gastric feeding tube, and other joys that filled most of 2008) that any basic lustiness we possessed plummeted. In the end, our relationship has become a kind of joyous, peaceful resting place. There's an inner contentment that comes from simply having time together, especially after we'd thought all was lost.

Surely there's more to a good marriage than sex or even sleeping together.

"Bill keeps a bed in his home office," Alice continues. "I don't sleep for more than a couple hours at a time due to spasms, so he sleeps in his separate bed a lot. It puts stress on our relationship."

Hold on, I start to say. I'm getting a mixed message here. What happened to greater empathy, a sharing of responsibilities, better fathering skills? "So, on balance," I finally come out with, "does the disability draw you together as a couple or push you apart? Is it a bridge or a wedge? Or neither?" I think it's becoming my favorite question.

Bill rejoins the conversation. "In some ways it's made us closer; in other ways it's a regular source of tension and stress."

"All in all," inserts Alice, "it's an obstacle."

The truth is probably somewhere in the middle. Or it fluctuates moment by moment.

Clearly, both Alice and Bill would like a medical breakthrough—or at least greater clarity about her prognosis. But when I ask about achievable changes, Bill has a short wish list. "Hire more outside help for cleaning, errands, etc."

Why don't they? Is it a matter of money? Maybe deep down they're just do-it-yourselfers. But it sounds as if they'd almost feel ashamed to hire help. To hire help is to admit you can't do it all yourself, and I'm not sure this couple has reached that point yet. From what Alice says next, I believe she's internally conflicted on the subject. Which I understand. Early in our marriage, M.L. was uncomfortable about hiring a weekly housekeeper. She didn't grow up with one. Her mother did everything. And sometimes we still fantasize about firing all the help and going it alone. But we know better.

"I'd love to have someone in to clean the house regularly," Alice is saying. "I can't do the heavy housework, and some days I can't cook dinner. I hate when he comes home to a messy house after working all day and stressing about me on top of it. I'd love to be able to have someone do the grocery/Costco shopping/walk the dog—to take that off his plate as well. . . . I wish I could take over the household accounts, [but I'm] too brain-foggy at times, which hurts even more because I have a finance degree. I'd like to be able to take my daughter somewhere, just the two of us."

Here's what I'm gleaning: Bill would understandably like a respite from his labors, while Alice sounds like what she seeks most is a reprieve from her guilty feelings.

"There are many times I wish I could give him a break from me—that I was strong enough for just one day to drive myself somewhere for a few hours [and] give him the house to himself," she laments.

A break from me. It sits there a moment in the dead air between us, like a malodorous ghost.

"Wouldn't a personal-care assistant help?" I press.

They exchange a look. "Bill's been alone as my caregiver for a really long time, and we've basically figured out most of this stuff on our own," she says.

It's a matter of pride. I understand—after all, M.L. and I have solved many of our problems by ourselves—but that doesn't mean we don't hire personal-care and household help. Sometimes I've had to insist on it, because I know M.L. can't do it all, even if she doesn't always want to admit it. I suppose all couples have to work out such decisions on their own terms. For Alice and Bill, this is still a work in progress.

Then something else occurs to me: maybe there's a sort of upside. I mean, being stuck in bed could be . . . comfortable. "Can you read? Watch TV? Sleep? Pet the cat?" I ask later. (Actually, they don't have a cat, but Alice's "giant goofy Lab-mix [is] glued to my side on flare days," she says.)

I don't want my inquiry to sound flippant or accusatory. Perhaps I'm trying to lighten the mood, find the silver lining. In truth, I'd hate to be stuck in bed. When I have been—with the flu or recovering from surgery, say—I've become intimately familiar with the mind-numbing frustration and boredom, not to mention stubborn, painful pressure sores.

"I spend a lot of time on Facebook and Twitter," she answers. "The Internet is my saving grace lately." She messages with friends all day long, "living vicariously through them," she says. "I write when I'm stressed, but it takes up a lot of mental energy that gets drained by brain fog most of the time." Ditto her reading enjoyment. "I love reading . . . but my comprehension gets wiped by brain fog. There are periods when I can't read at all." The neurological issues associated with EDS can make her vision fuzzy too. So she listens to a lot of soft music. She's become extremely sensitive to boisterous intonations, though—sometimes even the sound of close conversation can be physically painful. "I've taken up meditation," she says. "I started seeing a really good pain therapist and have been learning a lot. It's something I can do every day, no matter what, without fail. Pretty much the only thing."

I feel as though I've just asked a Holocaust survivor to tell me something cheerful about the camps. Still, I ask, "What about assistive devices?" I'm thinking of tray tables that work with beds, remote controlled lights and windows, voice-controlled gadgets, and the like.

She says she doesn't use equipment of that nature much, yet. "I have a ton of pillows and have made my bed as comfortable as I can—and it's really freaking comfortable!—but as for assistive devices, I'm doing okay without, for now. When I used to faint multiple times a day, I used a wheelchair and a shower chair."

Again, maybe I'm trying too hard to extract good news. I remember that during those long months I was stuck in a hospital bed I had no greater joy than when my daughters would come in and watch TV with me. I didn't care what the show was. I became absurdly fond of an Australian series about a group of young mermaids that enthralled my younger daughter. The way she would sing along to the theme song made my eyes tear.

When she can, Alice does watch TV with her family. "Hannah and I watch *So You Think You Can Dance*, *Planet Earth*, *American Idol*, and various other things together. It's a good way to get some snuggle time in. Bill and I have shows that we watch together as well, but a lot of the time I'm just in too much pain to interact with anyone."

"Do you expect these flare-ups to get worse in the years ahead?" I say. I'm hoping, of course, she'll say no.

"It's all up in the air at this point. . . . I will always have complications from the EDS, and my connective tissue will continue to degrade. I will always have loose joints and be prone to injuries. I'm developing arthritis. But honestly, no doctor can tell me for sure. The research just isn't there yet."

Alice's disorder may be rare, but I believe that a lot of people with disabilities feel the same way she does about the lack of solutions offered by the medical establishment. How many times have doctors told me, "You're an exception . . . an unusual case!"? It continues to amaze me how little doctors know and how wrong they can be at times (or as I like to put it, "Doctors don't know shit!"). We truly have to learn about our own conditions, often through trial and error. We have to become our own health-care advocates. As a result, we often become world experts on our diagnoses and their implications.

The Lawsons are facing Alice's mysterious, unpredictable limitations—the plural is especially appropriate here—with concerted determination and intelligence, as I like to think M.L. and I do. They present a united front, as I believe we do. Most of the time.

Just the other night, because of a cold I've been fighting for too long, I had a bad mucous plug obstruct my breathing. This happens occasionally and is common among people like me. I'd had my attendant try to suction it out earlier in the day—I'd trained him how to use the little catheter-vacuum device we'd acquired after my hospitalization for the colostomy surgery and now use only when necessary—with limited success. By dinnertime the obstruction had grown scary. The attendant had gone home, and M.L., now a skilled suctioner, tried and tried to clear my airways. Every trick we could think of—drinking water, eating food, nebulizing with a bronchodilator and expectorant—failed to produce the desired result. (I have a CoughAssist machine, which is supposed to help by automatically filling the lungs with air and then sucking back like a vacuum, to artificially induce a strong cough, but I've never found it to do any good.)

So into the evening we kept suctioning, hour after hour without success. Desperate and exhausted, I finally had her lay me down in bed and roll me around, another maneuver for loosening stubborn phlegm. For a moment there, sweaty and tousled, I almost thought I could cough the plug up myself. But I couldn't. With great patience, she tried the suction machine once again. This time, with the tubing midway to the bottom of my lungs, the noisy device stopped cold. She waited, held firm. The wad from inside my chest had plugged the appliance! Then, a moment later, it miraculously moved through the tube. My airways were clear at last! (Has anyone ever told you that oxygen can be delicious?)

I owe M.L. my life many times over, it's true. It's equally true, I believe, that we are a great team. We give each other strength, encouragement, and knowledge.

The next day, in our final talk, I hear a ray of hope in Alice Lawson's voice.

"There's a doctor at Stanford who's interested in my case," she tells me. This doctor thinks she might not have ever had POTS at all but, rather, a "cerebral spinal fluid leak due to tissue weakness from the EDS, contributing to tears in the dura of my spinal cord."

I think I know what she means, more or less. The EDS had caused a rupture in the connective tissue around her spine, which in turn caused drainage akin to a spinal tap.

She goes on: "So I'll be going to Stanford with Bill for extensive testing and perhaps treatment, which could make some of the POTS issues disappear. It's a long shot, but we're going to try." The underlying EDS is not in question, she clarifies, but if this doctor's hunch is right, she could regain some of her old active lifestyle. "I'm hopeful yet realistic," she says. "He has patients who have had their brain fog, GI issues, headaches, and POTS symptoms cured."

"Fingers crossed," I reply—which I can't actually do physically, but the phrase conveys my hopefulness. I ask her to keep me posted.

Maybe that's the best we can realistically hope for, to be a loose-knit mutual support club. A network, a village. We can't always find surefire answers or solutions or cures, but we can vent and validate and crowdsource, and, if nothing else, wish one another strength and courage. Sometimes camaraderie and understanding go a long way. And the sense of optimism they can bring may prove sufficient to carry us through another day.

FELICIA AND JUAN

◆

ANOTHER THIRTY-SOMETHING MARRIED couple provides a completely different take on life—and I almost blow our first interview.

Felicia and Juan Hernandez (not their real names) live in Scottsdale, Arizona. Juan was born with osteogenesis imperfecta, a congenital condition that gives him extremely brittle bones and makes him barely three feet tall. Nevertheless, he has sufficient strength to propel his small wheelchair with riveting power and grace. I soon learn he is, as my aged father might say, a character.

Felicia, his wife of four years, is fit and healthy-looking and outdoorsy—a passionate speaker with long flowing auburn hair and the glowing unlined face of an eighteen-year-old (she freely admits to being thirty-seven).

They are motivational speakers and life coaches, though those aren't the terms they prefer. Rather, they like to be called "entrepreneurs."

We'd scheduled a Skype session for a Friday afternoon, but I forgot about it until an e-mail marked *High Importance* arrives with the message "are you there?" Maybe the pleasant spring air had caused my mind to wander. Maybe I wasn't really looking forward to the conversation. You see, I'd completed some background research about Felicia and Juan. Consider this from Felicia's website:

> *The world is waiting for you:*
>
> · *To pursue your dreams and build them into your reality.*
> · *To live boldly and with self-confidence.*
> · *To do everything you were meant to do.*

And from Juan's: "Your heart is the roadmap to being your best self. Turn on your headlights and get going. Rock your world!" (Cue the heavy-metal guitar?)

I'll admit that I've altered the website content to protect Felicia and Juan's anonymity. But you get the picture. Both sounded so corny to me, so pretentious and phony.

Note to self: never judge people by their websites again.

Indeed, to my surprised delight Felicia and Juan turn out to be a sweet and truly engaging couple. Juan verily struts through life, if that word can be applied to someone so short and on wheels, and he's a champion at making faces. He raises and lowers his thick eyebrows with abandon, and his tongue constantly flicks across his smiling lips. At thirty-six, he shaves his head bald and sports a scruffy soul patch. What's most noticeable is his perpetual devilish grin, and his face is further punctuated by eyes as bright and twinkly as halogen bulbs.

"It's actually very complementary, what we do," Felicia is explaining. Her voice is so sonorous, so clear, that she could be a pitchwoman for an exercise program or a beauty product. She's also that charismatic and convincing. "Juan is primarily a speaker," she's saying. "He'll do keynotes all over the world, and he runs his own events, but he also does some one-on-one coaching and therapy. I'm more involved in the coaching side"—her specialty is intensive, individualized life-skills training—"but I've also spoken on stages around the world. We have some clients who cross over back and forth between us, because the programs are so complementary."

Juan stays quiet for the moment. His official training is as a hypnotherapist. He's certified by the American Board of Hypnotherapy and holds a doctorate in clinical hypnosis. But he's also a self-trained entertainer, skilled at ensnaring a crowd with his energy and charm, and holding them captive. With a voice that's somewhat high-pitched but projects with the assurance of an experienced actor's (I've seen his clips), he might start a presentation by explaining that he decided at an early age to treat his disability as a gift rather than a burden. He set out on a mission to tell the world that life is what you make of it, that your destiny is in your hands. To my chagrin, when I hear Juan deliver his spiel online, I find I'm holding my breath in rapt attention.

Felicia, perched beside him now, is saying with a deliberate, sharply enunciated diction that it was their shared business interests that brought them together in the first place. In 2008, a mutual friend suggested she connect with Juan on Facebook because they were in the same industry. More than a year passed before they met in person, at a conference in Juan's hometown of Chicago. After the conference, she returned home to Portland, Oregon, but they kept in touch. "We were friends. But he definitely did not want to be in the friend zone," she recalls.

"I wasn't really interested in having more friends," Juan tells me. "I already had enough women friends." From his mouth, that sounds like innuendo. He could almost play a short-statured Groucho.

Felicia chuckles. She likes his innuendo. "His intentions were fairly clear, but he'd just come out of a bad relationship, and I didn't think he was ready to jump into a new one." In time, though, he talked her into visiting him in Chicago. That was in the spring of 2010. "From that point forward, there were great sparks," she says.

"We had immediate chemistry," Juan insists. "We had so much in common, and I had complete confidence we weren't going to stay just friends."

I ask about her initial impression of his disability. Her publicity material says she's "an award-winning humanitarian"—she's won a fellowship for her work with women and children in Africa, six months of which had to do with HIV and AIDS prevention in Kenya and Uganda. She's also earned an MFA in creative writing from Pacific University and a PhD in metaphysics (the latter she downplays, she tells me later, fearing "metaphysics" sounds too weird). But she'd had no experience with people with disabilities before meeting Juan. "I'd actually never heard of osteogenesis imperfecta. I didn't really have any preconceived notions either way."

A few months later, after the visit, Felicia moved to Chicago, where she had family, primarily to be nearer to Juan. A year afterward they were engaged, and in 2012 they married.

The next time we talk, Juan has laryngitis, so he writes answers to my questions on an iPad. I ask how he feels about my calling him "a person with a disability." Perhaps he favors "Little Person" or "Person of Short Stature," as some people with dwarfism I've known do. He shakes his head and scribbles furiously:

> I don't identify with labels—except for the parking privileges. :) Dis-able means NOT-ABLE, not an accurate depiction of me. I say I'm 3' tall and use a wheelchair for mobility.

I understand. "Use a wheelchair" is a term I favor too. I remember fighting for it years ago to replace "wheelchair-bound" and "confined to a wheelchair," both of which seemed to imply limitation, an outmoded view of life on wheels. I wrote letters to the editors of various magazines and newspapers, many of which got printed. That was my introduction to activism. I believe it's important for marginalized people to be able to set their own terms of identity. Still, I can't help thinking Juan doesn't want to be part of any movement and doesn't have a lot of contact with other disabled folks. The fact that he dislikes the word "disability" is the first clue that he doesn't identify with the larger cause. Plus, he never talks about disability politics or policies. He doesn't attend disability-rights conferences. He doesn't seem clued in to what other disability activists are doing.

It turns out I'm right, but only later will I discover how Juan justifies his go-it-alone attitude.

In one of his early presentations—when he still had tufts of brown hair—Juan comes out on stage in his wheelchair and tells the audience about a childhood ambition. Specifically, he talks about the day he told his teachers he'd decided he was going to be president some day! "Do you think they said, 'Oh, yes, you *are*!'?" he asks the crowd, imitating a kindergarten teacher's condescending tone. Pause. "Do you think they said that—yes or no?" Another pause. Someone in the audience giggles. "No! You know what they said? They said, 'Oh, sweetie'"—he shakes his head—"'pump the brakes. I mean, maybe, like, a congressman . . . ?'"

It's a funny bit of shtick. His point, of course, is that he didn't receive the same kinds of encouragement as other little boys simply because of his physical differences. That hurt, he admits, for a time. Then he decided not to listen to naysayers, not to accept their artificial limitations on his potential. He became the incarnation of gumption and true grit.

"Inspiration porn" is a phrase that's been brought up in connection with Juan's activities. The charge is that he exploits his disability to make other people feel sorry for him and then, when they least expect it, feel inspired. In disability politics, it's tantamount to accusing him of being a performing monkey. I don't like the idea of dividing people with disabilities into different castes according to their enlightenment, limitations, or approaches to life, but the description strikes me as not entirely inaccurate in Juan's case. He is presenting himself as an inspiration—an inspiration for no other reason than that he has refused to accept the discouragement and cosseting of others. This achievement is really not so unusual or inspiring in the world of people with disabilities, considering that's what most survivors do on a daily basis.

In a subsequent chat, I ask Juan if he knows the term "inspiration porn" and whether he thinks it makes any sense when people use it about him and his presentations. He replies without missing a beat: "It does make sense, and people can say whatever they want about me." He smiles broadly, that lizard's tongue flashing. "I'm doing my *thang*, and have been for twenty-two years—professionally! I take heat on all kinds of shit. Whatevs."

Okay, I'm a little irritated by his blasé attitude, but I suspect this insouciance is the source of his inner strength and outward power. Besides, it's hip not to respond to or engage with "haters," right? Brushing off criticism is considered a sign not of superficiality but of self-confidence, of an independent spirit. And both of those traits he seems to have in abundance.

As I look at Juan's compact yet beefy frame, I believe I'm beholding the merger of a person and his persona. He can't shake off the onstage swagger, at least not for me. I must remember that Juan *is* a performer. He soaks up adulation for conveying indomitability, for telling jokes and engaging—not challenging—his audiences. Why shouldn't he use the assets he was born with? Why shouldn't he take control of the message and charge people for it? That's what the freak-show performers of old used to say, many of whom were Little People, who as a group have had a long career in showbiz: "Let people stare, as long as they pay for the privilege!"

But Juan's story has a kind of secret I soon unearth. His persona as a man who redefined himself and achieved a high degree of independence is somewhat of a sham. Or at least it was, until Felicia came into his life.

It wasn't just their shared entrepreneurial interest in motivational speaking and life coaching that fueled Juan and Felicia's union. In a sense, his disability became part of the magic between them. "Juan is fairly independent," says Felicia now. Juan nods in agreement. "He really can access everything on his own. He doesn't drive, but pretty much everything else—personal hygiene, getting ready in the morning, working, working out—he can do independently."

He couldn't, however, when they met. Even while he was on the motivational-lecture circuit, hosting events and rousing people to get out of their own way and maximize their potential, he was still living with his parents in an inaccessible home where he had no independence.

"His father would carry him in from the car to a wheelchair that resided on the first floor. But his bedroom was on the second floor, so he had to be carried upstairs every night," Felicia relates.

He moved about his bedroom by scooting around the floor with his hands. The bed was on the floor, so he could move in and out of bed but couldn't shower or get food on his own. Felicia was surprised by the arrangement, and together they devised ways to empower him to greater independence.

The house they now share is on one level. The accessible bathroom has a roll-in shower and a toilet onto which he can transfer himself. The house also has two kitchens—a "regular" one for Felicia and a separate, shorter one in which Juan can reach the refrigerator, the grill, the toaster oven, the water faucet, and all the cooking utensils. "None of that stuff he had in the past," she says.

But I'm still not getting how this monumental transformation actually occurred.

"It was a combination," says Felicia, "of me saying, 'You can have this independence, and you should because it's really fun to have freedom and independence,' and Juan's creativity about figuring out what'll work."

Juan makes one of his funny raised-eyebrow faces and says, "Felicia was the coolest woman I'd ever met, so I knew I had to mature quickly to keep a woman like her." He concedes he was reluctant about these lifestyle changes at first. "I didn't believe it was possible, and I didn't know I'd like it so much, this independence," he says. His biggest fear was that he was too fragile to be autonomous. "I knew a bunch of people at the OI Foundation," he explains, referring to a large charitable organization for people with osteogenesis imperfecta, "and most of the ones I knew who had more independence didn't fracture as often as I do." In other words, they had a less disabling form of OI.

His parents had been overprotective too. They traveled with him everywhere—they thought it was important to show him the world—but they never put much effort into creating an accessible environment for him.

"That's what they chose," says Felicia with a shrug. "To me, where you live should be the most important thing. I'm always an advocate for, What else can we do to make life more accessible?"

She put her can-do attitude to work for Juan. But this brings me up short. I wouldn't want someone poking and prodding to make my life better. Though, when I was younger, I do recall complaining that M.L. didn't bug and push me enough. At that point I wanted someone to tell me what to do, to be my external engine. What I wanted then, I've assumed ever since, was actually a replacement for my mother. To grow up, I figured I had to learn to be my own man. And ever since, I've been grateful for *not* having a nagging spouse.

Not that Felicia is a nagger. Talking with her and Juan, I'm put in mind of the movie cliché of the disabled vet who feels sorry for himself, and only the love and encouragement of a good woman can bring him out of his shell. (See the post–World War II classic *The Best Years of Our Lives*.) I didn't think relationships ever happened like that in real life. I thought most of us had to self-actualize and, if anything, convince others that we're more than we might appear. Maybe Juan was just looking for a viable escape from his overprotective parents, and Felicia provided a way.

"If you had no background in disabilities, how did you know what to do?" I ask Felicia. "How did you know what would work?"

Juan chortles. He didn't know it would work, he says. Felicia says it was just "a matter of getting creative around what can make life better." But I suspect they also plied their professional trade on each other, nudging each other to maximize potential.

✦ ✦ ✦

"Earlier in my life, I didn't have as much balance and strength as I have now, physically speaking," Juan tells me during our next talk. "So that also impacted what I was able to do. I mean, we're still learning as we go, but I'm in better shape now physically as well as emotionally."

I ask him to explain how he came to improve his balance and strength. Is that related to physical exercise? "Yes, but it's probably even more to do with mindset," says Felicia, since Juan is still hoarse. She tells me how, not long after they moved to Scottsdale, she sat him up on a low wall to take in the vista and be closer to her standing height. He may not depend on her for daily care, but he's easy for her to lift. She remembers noticing the way he gripped her tightly so as not to fall. Now, she's sure, that wouldn't happen. He would sit there easily, confidently, with no anxieties about falling.

"Self-trust," he croaks out. "I trust my body more now, because I know what it feels like in different positions and situations."

"Before all this," she says, leaning in, "he would sit either in his wheelchair or on the floor, which is obviously very safe. You can't fall off the floor! But now his comfort level is higher in a variety of situations."

Felicia's motivation for improving Juan's self-confidence and independence is twofold: one, she thinks it's best for him; two, she doesn't want him to be overly dependent on her. "I don't want you to have to wait for me to do it for you," she says, turning to Juan, "because I'm busy, and I have other things to do. So if we can figure out a way to have him do it himself," she continues, angling her head back toward me, "that's better all around. We just try out different things until we find something that works."

But there are risks. Two years ago Juan was training a service dog. It was still a puppy, not yet disciplined to obey instructions and ignore distractions. Juan took the dog across the street to the mailbox. "Bad idea," he stage-whispers to me.

Another small dog started yipping at Juan's dog. In response, Juan's puppy ran after the other dog at breakneck speed. Juan was gripping the leash, and the force pulled his chair over and propelled Juan face-first onto the cement.

Because Juan has brittle bones, he fractured much of the right side of his body. Most of the next week was spent in the hospital on morphine. That stay was followed by nearly three months of recovery at home. Felicia took care of him, aided by Juan's parents, who flew in from Chicago, and assorted neighbors and friends. They stayed at his bedside practically round-the-clock until he was able to get himself around again. "We would either just sit with Juan or help him go to the bathroom or whatever. He literally wasn't able to move at all. So it was a kind of team effort between me and whoever was around to work all that out. For the first month, he lost his short-term memory too, which wasn't fun."

More recently, Juan was in a car accident. He was a passenger in a car with five of his students when a semitruck pulled out in front of them on the highway. There wasn't enough time or space to stop, and Juan's car crashed into it. They all managed to get away with only minor injuries.

"Maybe your parents were right to be protective," I say, going for an easy laugh myself. Then, not sure my remark was appropriate, I follow with: "Or do you feel they were neglectful about your access needs?"

"Depends who you ask" is all Juan says on that subject.

But Felicia insists they have a great relationship today. Juan's father is his business partner. They talk every few days about marketing strategies and other, more personal matters. "Juan's parents are still somewhat overprotective," she says, "but they also get that he's an adult and living separately now. They've seen how great independence looks on him and how happy he is with all the things he can do. So they're supportive and much more hands-off than they used to be, even though I think their tendency is still toward being overprotective."

I can't help wondering if she feels a rivalry with Juan's parents. Felicia almost makes it sound as if Juan is her pet project. I realize I need to dig a little deeper to better understand the dynamics of their relationship.

When we talk again, I ask about the give-and-take between them. It's obvious what Felicia has done for Juan, I say—helping him move out of his parents' house, enabling him to find his independence—but what does he give her?

"I tend to take things very seriously," Felicia answers. "I'm committed to achieving certain goals I set for my life. And Juan adds a lot of laughter, levity, and fun to my life and to our relationship. We call him our CFO because he's our Chief Fun Officer—that's how he likes to live. He likes things to be fun, and he likes to be funny. That's one of my favorite things about our relationship."

Juan moves forward in his wheelchair. "Ask *me* what I give her."

"Okay," I bite. "You have something to add?"

"Sex!"

They both chuckle. I'm not sure what to make of this. She's neither offended by nor wholeheartedly encouraging of Juan's potty mouth. She's used to it, I gather. But then she abruptly returns to a serious tone. His commercial acumen, she says, has helped her business. "Juan has added a ton of value [to my business] because he has a great network of connections and really cool ideas. We talk all the time about different marketing strategies."

She's all business. I can see that. But marketing strategies toward what goal? Where to from here? What's their long-term plan or dream?

Felicia straightens in her chair, conveying the importance of what she says next. "Our next big goal is to buy a more accessible house," she says. "We've made our current living space as accessible as possible, but it wasn't technically an accessible house to start with. The doorways and hallways are standard width, not extra wide for a wheelchair. The light switches are too high for him to reach without sticks, which is how he turns on the lights now."

They plan to either buy a place that's already accessible or to build one. It's a nice domestic image, and I'm warmed by the lovely picture she's painting. But I've been an activist and can't help thinking that access barriers are a political cause, not just an individual challenge. You can look for a home that meets your needs, but have you considered why so many places don't? "It's partly a disability rights issue," I say tentatively, wondering if they've thought about working toward a more enlightened world with fewer architectural barriers in the first place.

They nod in unison. Juan volunteers, "I've been asked sometimes to do disability speeches and things like that, but I tend not to go for those."

"Why not?"

"I find those groups are too militant, or there's a lot of pity there, or they're just angry, you know?"

I understand what he's saying. But still, those groups do a lot of good. That's not Juan's style, though. He's nonconfrontational and steadfastly nonserious.

Then, perhaps sensing I might be annoyed by what Juan's just said—or recognizing that Juan himself has benefited from the efforts of some of those militant angry people—Felicia pipes up with, "They're in the mode of fighting for those rights, which is important, of course. Very important. But the attitude they carry, Juan doesn't really resonate with."

I like Juan and Felicia, despite my knee-jerk cynicism, but I do wish he'd embrace the cause, use a portion of his influence to make life better for myriad others who might not have heard of him. Insist on access in public places. Protest injustice. Call out the "bad actors," whether corporations or politicians or individuals who block full integration of folks on wheels or with other types of disabilities.

But then again, there are full-time activists who could say the same of me. Let's face it, political demonstrations just don't suit everybody.

✦   ✦   ✦

I round out our final Skype chat with a cornball question: Ever thought about having children? "We get asked that all the time" is Felicia's response. "At this point, we're not closed off to the idea . . . but we're not in a rush either."

I make supportive noises to signify understanding, but really, that's the sort of diplomatic answer you'd give your grandma. Of course, what I really wonder about is how they imagine coping with parenthood from a disability perspective.

"We're too selfish with our time . . . and sleep," says Juan. He's lasered in on something I was thinking. Felicia and Juan are too preoccupied with their own lives and businesses to have time for children. I try to confirm this.

"Our businesses are our babies," says Felicia. "We work with so many clients, and it's almost like they're our kids." She adds that she's also not averse to adopting, which is one way to ignore her biological clock. She's spent time in Africa, after all, and seen many parentless children. "We would be phenomenal parents," she says, "and there are a lot of kids out there that could use good families, that could be adopted."

Juan punctuates this topic with characteristic comicality. "But I like to practice making babies," he says with a lascivious smirk.

We all giggle, even though it makes me feel like I'm ten years old.

"And after that?" I prompt.

"Take over the world!" Juan says.

Felicia clears her throat and says they'd like to keep doing what they're doing. "We really love it, and love and adore the clients we get to work with. I don't see that changing." They like Scottsdale too. It's "handicap friendly," she says, which she then defines as flat and snowless, with lots of accessible parking. Juan nods, for once zingerless.

"But tell me," I say, "what could you do better?" My stomach twists like a pretzel hearing myself ask this question. One hates to nitpick, to be the uncool one, but I'm trying to establish that this couple isn't really as self-serving as they may sound.

They're staring back at me, and the silence is deafening.

"What's the best thing you've done, then—a presentation or one-on-one or whatever?" I say.

"The last one I did," answers Juan. "That's always my motto." Then he asks me, "Do you have love in your life?"

Momentarily bewildered at becoming the questioned, I explain that I've been married twenty-six years to a nondisabled woman and we have two daughters. Juan seems pleased, particularly at the duration of my marriage.

"Do people think your wife is your nurse or sister?" he asks then.

"All the time," I say, feeling a shift in the ether between us, a deeper connection established through the magic of Skype. At that moment I hear M.L. come in, home from work. She waves and tiptoes to the kitchen.

"Us too," says Juan. "How do you handle that?"

"It depends," I say. "But I should be asking *you* that. How do you handle it?" He shrugs. I answer my own question to fill the silence. "Sometimes we ignore it," I say. "Sometimes we shake our heads and shrug it off. Sometimes we get angry. But probably at our best moments we'll stop and explain to people, make it a teachable moment."

M.L., overhearing, shouts from the kitchen, "Don't wear white shoes."

I repeat this into my microphone. "I get it," says Felicia triumphantly. "So I don't look like a nurse." This time we've made *them* laugh.

Maybe they've worked their magic on me, but I realize my doubting heart has melted. I realize Juan's upbeat personality and seeming unflappability remind me of a younger version of myself, an overconfident overachiever who would deflect unpleasant thoughts and feelings with barbed humor. It'd served me well for years, pretending to be brave, trivializing my fears and limitations. Perhaps that youthful refusal to see myself as a victim is something I've lost sight of—that cocksure wheelchair strut. When, I wonder, did troubles stop rolling off my back? Was it when I turned forty? Fifty? Why so self-serious, fearful, and unsure these days? If you treat life like a carnival, does it become one? Is that something people who hide or bury their disability consciousness, their rage at an unjust world, have over the rest of us? And is it too late to regain that level of self-assuredness?

With so many questions buffeting my brain, I thank Felicia and Juan for their time. But for me, that's not the end of the connection. A few months later, I get back in touch to ask if they'd like to review a draft of their chapter (I'm giving everyone a chance to correct goofs and misunderstandings). They decline. They trust me, they say. "Best of luck, bud," says Juan, a dude to the end.

And I'm pleased to have earned their trust, to be Juan's bud.

LAURIE AND TIM

—◆—

I'VE ALWAYS FELT FORTUNATE. That may surprise some people. It surprised M.L. when I first mentioned it to her. But I'm fortunate, I insist, to have been born when I was and where I was, with a sense of privilege in a time of relative peace and prosperity. And fortunate in the financial sense too.

Yes, I was born with an incurable "muscle-wasting disease," as the Muscular Dystrophy Association used to put it. Plus, my parents split up when I was nine, my mother died when I was just eighteen . . . and so forth. But all of those potential setbacks would've been much more devastating had I not been born into an educated family that possessed intelligence, a sense of honesty and decency, and—let's face it—monetary resources.

The difference between having and not having is particularly crucial for people with disabilities. It can be the difference between being able to get out of bed in the morning or being completely stuck there. Between comfort and pain. Sometimes between being able to breathe and, well, being dead. To a crip, adequate resources and support systems can mean everything.

When I went off to Harvard, which was a fortunate opportunity in itself, I did so with great self-assurance—or so I convinced myself—that I could live independently in a freshman dorm and, later, in one of the storied "Houses" (Harvard's residential quarters for second-, third-, and fourth-year students) with a live-in attendant. That's a self-confidence that perhaps only money and encouragement can buy. Several lying, stealing, disappearing, alcohol- and drug-abusing attendants later, I felt shaken and unsure. But I knew the idea was good, the concept that I should be able to live on my own, under my own direction, if only my myriad custodial needs were met. And the only way I could meet those needs was if Dad kept sending checks. (Now that I'm old enough to acknowledge his largesse as a gift and not my due, my heartfelt gratitude scarcely registers as adequate.)

My abiding good fortune is what flashes through my mind when I first meet Laurie and Tim Young of Edmonton, Alberta, Canada, for reasons which will become apparent.

Laurie, forty-five, was born with SMA, like Shane and Kevin and yours truly. But she was born with one very important difference: she's Canadian. Tim, fifty-three, is able-bodied. They've been married nineteen years.

Laurie and Tim aren't rich, but they have all they need. That's what they tell me. Our first conversation is by e-mail. Laurie writes that her sister, who also has SMA, inadvertently introduced her and Tim. "She worked with Tim, and they were all heading out for drinks one evening and invited me along. It's sort of funny—she was trying to set Tim up with another woman. He got me instead."

Later, I ask Tim about that night. "What first attracted you to Laurie, and what then made you go the extra step of tying the knot?"

"It was her sense of humor," he says. "To this day, all I have to do is see her smile and I feel happy. Laurie's got a smile that's just amazing."

And I can see that she smiles often. They both do. They tease each other and joke. It's a warm kind of interplay.

Laurie is a youthful-looking woman with a round face framed by smooth black hair. Sitting in her motorized wheelchair—which, I note, doesn't include a head-support, indicating a degree of neck strength I myself haven't had since childhood—she is at most five feet tall. Her arms bear colorful tattoos, thirteen tats in all, she tells me, representing big moments in her life, such as a portrait of Scooter, a dog they lost; a palm tree, to commemorate their many happy vacations to sunny climes; and a purple rose in memory of a friend with SMA who died. Her feet show the edema that's common among those of us who sit all day, and she has scoliosis. Otherwise, she's neither emaciated nor rag-doll floppy, the two camps many of us muscle-less SMAers tend to fall into. (My older brother used to compare me to the Pillsbury doughboy, before my big weight loss in puberty brought on my current scrawny demeanor.) Laurie, in contrast, appears distinctly healthy.

Tim puts his muscular arm around her sloping shoulders. He's a vigorous, hardy-looking man who speaks slowly, carefully, and with great sincerity. Though he's eight years older than Laurie, he doesn't look it. It's plain that he adores and dotes on her. "We hit it off right away," he says now.

She was a working woman living independently with paid assistants. I ask if her disability was an issue of any kind in his feelings for her. "Not even a little bit," he answers.

Growing up, Tim had a quadriplegic uncle—from a car accident—with whom he used to go on excursions. Over the years he'd helped the uncle with all aspects of his care. But he'd never dated anyone with a disability before Laurie.

"We were engaged after three months," she says. "If it's meant to be, why wait? We were married a year later." She was twenty-six and he thirty-four.

Perhaps I'm reading too much into Laurie's comments, but many of us with a degenerative condition don't like to waste time. Diagnosed at age two, Laurie had dated since she was fourteen and had her first serious boyfriend in high school. It was a regular high school, and the boyfriend was not disabled. "We were together for two years," she says. On through college, she "dated a lot and honestly had a great time. I spent a lot of time at clubs and always got asked to dance. . . . I'm sure there were guys who didn't want to date me because of my disability, but I didn't have time to worry about them."

She says her friends were comfortable lifting her into cars and folding the manual wheelchair she used in those days into the back. She never felt left out socially. Sexually, however, she says she was "pretty innocent" before age seventeen. (*Seventeen?!* I was innocent till nineteen, and many other crips I know were innocent well into their twenties!) "On par with my able-bodied friends," she reflects.

Her sense of belonging may have come from her affluent upbringing (though she's not affluent now), or it may have existed in spite of that. Her parents, she's quick to tell me, didn't approve of Tim. That's partly because he was a divorcé. "They were worried about protecting their assets," she says. (Which reminds me of the remark someone made in the early years of my relationship with M.L.—that I must be rich, because there was no other conceivable reason why an able-bodied woman would be with someone like me.) "My parents didn't speak to me for six months."

"They're not the greatest people," Tim puts in. "They treat her like she doesn't belong."

"I thought it was *you* they didn't like," I say.

"They don't, or they didn't. But over the years, they've tried to get me to talk to her about things they don't like—such as her tattoos," he says. "I've got one myself, so why'd they think I'd say something about that—except maybe, get more! I support the things she does." He recounts a recent visit during which he actually had to kick her father out of their house. "He called Laurie fat and tried to get me to make her eat less."

Fat-shaming seems particularly cruel when directed at someone who's incapable of aerobic exercise, but I don't say anything beyond, "Hmm . . ."

Tim's family, on the other hand, has been more accommodating—except for his eight brothers, whom Laurie calls "alcoholic and dysfunctional." Tim has another explanation: "They're intimidated by her intelligence," he says. "They lack class and respect—that's what I think."

Whatever the source of family discord, both agree it has nothing to do with her disability.

How different Laurie and Tim's life is from my own situation! From early on, my family-funded autonomy made my relationship with M.L. possible, and that fiscal support continues to undergird our lives today. Without it, I might not have felt entitled to all the same rights as anyone else: the right to date, to have sex, to work, to play, to marry. And, for that matter, without such a normal sense of self-worth I might not have been a terribly appealing romantic prospect.

In the first few years after M.L. and I moved to LA, I recall, Dad's support began to dwindle. The weekly check for the attendant became a monthly stipend for *all* expenses, including medical coverage (which, in those days, because of my "preexisting condition," was almost impossible to get on my own and, when I did manage to by joining an organization for freelance writers, was hugely expensive). I amassed enormous debt, something on the order of sixty thousand bucks, spread out over several credit cards in those go-go days when balance-transfer offers filled the mailbox like manna. I wasn't spending extravagantly. These debts were for legitimate expenses.

My financial woes were only resolved after my near-death hospitalization. I'm referring to the time in December 2007 when I entered Cedars-Sinai Medical Center for a routine check of my colon. I had ulcerative colitis that wasn't responding well to medication. The daily diarrhea and cramping were causing me to lose too much weight too fast. Little did I know I was about to drop another quarter of my body weight.

My intestines, it turned out, were mostly destroyed by an infection. When I awoke from early morning surgery, much of my colon had been removed, and in its place was a colostomy pouch. What I didn't know then was that the surgeon had also left me with an internal tear that was hemorrhaging badly.

More than a week passed in that hospital. I begged to be sent home. Finally, on Christmas Eve, the doctor agreed to my release. But then, at four a.m. the next day: excruciating gut pain. My new colostomy pouch filled with blood. M.L. dialed 911, and an ambulance whisked me to the emergency room at the nearer UCLA hospital. The girls had to spend Christmas morning on their own.

The last thing I remember before going black was being wheeled into a hospital room after several hours in the ER. When I awoke, it was like rising to the surface of a soupy pool. I had been dreaming I was on stage and the curtain was opening.

When the tubes were finally removed from my throat, I could speak but didn't make much sense. Intravenously I was being fed antibiotics and steroids and antivirals and God knows what else, making my brain numb. That went on for months.

But this much information got through: What had happened was I'd gone into septic shock from the internal hemorrhaging the original surgeon had left. I'd been in a coma. I now had a new colostomy pouch, resectioned and moved to the left side of my abdomen from the right. It wouldn't be the last mini coma I would be in either before I was able to eat food—solid or liquid—again. In all, the ordeal would last nine months and change my marriage forever.

For the first part of that ordeal, my family had gathered around. M.L. had called them away from vacation, said I was dying. It was true. She's not prone to exaggeration.

They helped in numerous and important ways. They took the girls to movies and restaurants. My younger brother, Jeff, answered my e-mails, made my excuses to work associates and friends alike. And my stepmother, Barbara, took care of the piling-up bills. (Dad had been generous, but he'd only earned an editor's salary, while Barbara had recently retired from a long and well-paid corporate career.) That's when she noticed the thousands we owed the credit card companies.

It may have been a thin silver lining, but my illness made a clearer statement of our financial predicament than anything I'd managed to convey to my family up till then. Not just the enormity of our debt but the legitimacy of our expenses. Medical insurance, doctor bills, wheelchair supplies, and, most of all, the attendants. Our moderate income—from my writing and editing work and the part-time retail job M.L. had taken after the girls were born—might've been enough for a decent life without these extraordinary costs, but it wasn't anywhere near enough for our real-world requirements.

Having seen our financial predicament in black and white, Barbara became our angel. Ever since, she's offered generous cash gifts when needed. She set up a trust, and any time we get in financial straits, I let her know, and the trust delivers. This arrangement remains in place today.

Debt gets under your skin and in your blood. After Barbara eased our financial problems and my body mended, life at home became calmer, happier, than it'd been before I'd gotten so sick. M.L. and I gained a new respect for each other, I believe. Not only did I owe her my life, but I'd caught a whiff of what exactly I gave her too, something I'd always been insecure about. I saw the way she'd forfeited most of her life during my hospitalization to looking after my well-being, without any resentment. I saw how much her life is tied up with mine, how our existences are braided together symbiotically. Maybe I give her a kind of motor, a context or purpose, but each of us needs the other to help establish a sense of direction, of identity. Call it codependent, but perhaps this is what keeps us on track, this intertwining of our methods and objectives. And the effect of these insights was to reveal a new timbre of trust and faith between us, a deeper love that's proved stronger and more passionate than youthful lust.

✦   ✦   ✦

Laurie and Tim tell me that, three years ago, she took early retirement from her full-time job as a case manager for an insurance company. She'd been responsible for worker's compensation claims, putting in ten-hour days interviewing claimants and writing reports. It was taking a toll, particularly since she was growing physically weaker—the natural gradual advancement of her disability. Yet her parents just didn't understand why she'd left a good job. "They blame me for the progression of my SMA," she says. "I have no idea *how* they can blame me for something out of my control, but now we are essentially estranged."

Laurie's decision to seek early retirement was aided and abetted by Tim. "The job was draining her energy, and she was just in a real bad place," he explains.

Tim still has his full-time job, in addition to providing the bulk of Laurie's personal care. He's an operations supervisor for the local paratransit system, Edmonton's Disabled Adult Transit Service, which provides door-to-door accessible vehicles for registered disabled folks.

"If I didn't have to work, I'd be Laurie's full-time aide," he says. "We like our privacy, and if we didn't need anybody else around, we'd prefer it."

Under their current system, Tim helps get Laurie up in the morning and back in bed at night. But for thirty-five hours a week, while he's at work, she has Ela come in and help. Ela finishes getting Laurie dressed, does her makeup and hair ("If I try to do it, she looks like a clown," says Tim), tends to laundry and other housework, does the grocery shopping, and drives Laurie anywhere she has to go. (Laurie has a van adapted to accommodate her wheelchair, but she can't drive herself.)

"We love Ela!" says Laurie. "Not only is she the most reliable person ever, but she even does Tim's laundry, which lessens the load on him."

Not all attendants will do that, I know. I recall one man I'd hired who insisted that M.L. and I divide our laundry because, he claimed, it was against his tribal traditions to touch women's underwear. (We still divide our laundry, but that's because she doesn't trust my attendants to wash her delicates without damaging them.) Another only made half the bed, to make it clear he didn't work for M.L., just me.

On weekends, Tim does everything for Laurie and around the house. My guilt about relying on M.L. too much is eased, hearing we're not the only ones with this kind of arrangement—though we do have a man who comes for two hours on weekend mornings, in addition to the one who comes eight hours a day during the week. Still, every morning M.L. sets me up (with a cup of coffee and my urinal, primarily), and every night she puts me to bed. That may change as we grow older, but for now we like this balance of assistance and privacy. It works for us.

I ask next about how they choose whom to hire. "She does the interviewing and selecting," says Tim, pointing at Laurie. "She's the one who spends the most time with the person. So she has to know what they're all about."

I smile. A*boot*. His Canadian accent is showing.

Our conversation is interrupted by a barking dog. They have two. The loud one is called Anderson Cooper. I laugh. (The other is Kailey.) Instead of children they have dogs. Laurie says she's not maternal ("I don't think it would be different if I didn't have SMA," she says), but she has become involved with animal rescue organizations. She also volunteers for the Canadian Red Cross and an international nonprofit called Families of Spinal Muscular Atrophy. Recently she's taken up writing, and Tim is encouraging her to write about her life.

I can't help wondering if Tim is trying too hard to be everything for Laurie. Later, I ask about this, and what she thinks she provides for *him*—the give-and-take that's less visible but deserves equal recognition. "Let me start by saying if it wasn't for me, we would NOT have a social life," she e-mails me, semiprivately. "I plan our frequent [get-togethers] with friends. I also help by managing our finances and making sure everything gets paid. All vacation planning and arranging is my job. Since I left full-time work, I also manage all the grocery shopping and the dogs' vet appointments. I think I also help him, as all wives should. I'm there to support him."

She gives an example. Two years ago Tim's mother died. "I spent twelve hours a day with him by her bedside. I sat with her when he needed a break," she says.

In our next conversation, a few weeks later, I revisit the issue with Tim. I ask if providing so much of Laurie's help ever becomes too much. I hesitate to use the word "burdensome" because it's a cliché about crips' mates I've heard too often.

"No," he says. "It makes us closer."

For him, the most nerve-racking times are when he can't be with her, he says, especially if she needs him. "If Laurie gets sick and I'm not here, that's stressful for me." A catch in his voice slows the conversation momentarily. "It doesn't happen often, but when it does, yeah. That's concerning."

Any stress that Tim does feel is relieved by simply walking the dogs, he says. He's clearly devoted to Laurie and her comfort. Being there for her has become his life's mission and biggest joy. That sounds noble and selfless, I point out. "Are you two church-goers?" I ask. "Or temple, mosque, whatever?"

"We're religious," Laurie answers, "in that we both believe in God. We don't attend church."

When I say they seem happy, Tim says, "Yup, we are," then jokes that some people think he's grumpy or unhappy. "People think I'm miserable, but it's just the way I come across. Deep down, I'm a real nice guy."

He chuckles, and I find myself laughing with him. But I wonder if it's that people assume anyone who looks after a disabled person so much must be miserable. That's certainly something M.L. has heard from strangers.

"We're both pretty strong," he goes on. "We depend on each other and try not to depend on others too much. So if she's not feeling well or something, she depends on me to help her, to be strong for her. And the same is true for me."

"But all couples fight sometimes," I challenge.

"True," he says. "You have to work through those things."

I take it a step further and ask, "How do you help her when you're angry, and by the same token how does she ask you for help when what she really wants is to run over your toes?" (Believe me, I know whereof I ask.)

Tim ponders my question for a beat or two. "Laurie might not like asking me for things, but the fact is she has to. I'd expect nothing less. If she didn't ask, then I *would* be really mad."

His words resonate. M.L. has said something similar to me. She needs to know I'm always truthful about whether I need help, not pretending to be stronger or more independent than I can be. She doesn't like it when I'm whiny, to be sure, but she needs clarity about when I do and don't require assistance. This gives her reassurance, so she doesn't have to interpret or second-guess. She doesn't have to feel guilty about missing a cue. This is part of the calculus of communication between us. Part of the code. *Our* code.

"You'd be mad if she didn't ask?" I repeat.

"I can't always read her mind," he says. "A lot of times I can, but not always. And if I don't know what she wants, I can't help her."

It's a simple lesson in honest communication, one all couples should learn. But the unbeliever in me can't quite accept that they're being totally honest with me or each other. No matter how deeply you're in love, open communication is a lot harder than Tim is making it sound. Isn't it?

In a subsequent chat, Laurie and Tim come around to acknowledging that, outside the necessities, they do have different interests and have worked out compromises. For instance, Tim is an outdoorsman. When they go camping, "there has to be a hotel or shopping center nearby for Laurie," he says. While Laurie might like to go to the movies, Tim is "not a big theater person," he admits. They're often at weekend farmers markets and enjoy going out of town in the accessible van. They once went as far as Kansas City, Missouri, sixteen hundred miles away from home. They'd like to go to Europe, but traveling by plane isn't easy. "I don't know how well she'd handle that," says Tim.

They have little in the way of future plans. "My hope in the next five or ten years? To be in the same place we're at now," says Tim. His words are a statement of contentment, not of a lack of ambition or imagination.

Yet he admits that he's afraid Laurie's disability will worsen. And he's afraid that aging may keep him from being able to continue providing what she needs. To protect Tim's back, Laurie already encourages him to use a Hoyer lift, a device for transferring someone from wheelchair to bed and vice versa using a hammock-like sling seat hooked to a kind of rotating boom on wheels. I rented one when M.L. was pregnant. She hated it. Adjusting the chains and fastenings, and pushing and steering the huge contraption against carpet resistance, proved more work than just lifting me bodily. Our bedroom wasn't quite big enough, anyway, and the thing requires a lot of clear space under the bed for adequate purchase. The sling has to be placed just right too, or you elevate crooked and risk falling out. So I understand exactly what Tim means when he says, "You have to waste a lot of time with the lifting device. And it looks so damn uncomfortable!"

"She's worried about your back," I remind him.

"I know. But let me worry about my own back."

This rugged individualism seems a running theme. "We both like our freedom," says Laurie.

I think I understand. It's no fun relying on others.

Yet I wonder how they can afford it—employing an attendant practically full-time, living on only one salary, and estrangement from family who might otherwise offer financial backup.

What Laurie tells me next floors me.

First, from her old insurance job she receives a pension of $4,000 Canadian a month, roughly $2,970 in the United States. On top of that, she gets another $4,500 Canadian ($3,340 US) a month for her attendant expenses—that is, self-directed, long-term home care provided by the government. "In Canada, medical-care funding, including home care, is not dependent on income, [and] there is no penalty for getting legally married," she says.

This, of course, is in contrast to the situation in the United States. More than once I've tried to cadge some government largesse. My income is low, my expenses high. What more do the feds need? Less, actually. Any liquid savings, outside home and car, amounting to more than $2,000 disqualifies you from federal and state aid programs for the disabled, including Supplemental Security Income (SSI), and Medicaid. For a married couple, the cutoff is $3,000, or just $1,500 per person. So I receive nothing.

Activists call these requirements the "marriage disincentive," and I would add that they also create a savings disincentive. I've been advised by attorneys and other knowledgeable, opinionated folks to liquidate all my assets, buy a huge house if necessary (and perhaps take in a boarder), just so I'll qualify for benefits. But doing so would leave me completely at the mercy of the government, which is far too perilous for my comfort. Many disabled people are in this exact predicament, of course, and they are among the most strident and righteous advocates for systemic change. For them, advocacy is nothing less than a matter of survival. I'm financially more secure, thankfully, but I support these patriots with all my heart and voice. Why should the government force us to go broke (and stay single) in order to secure the very expensive resources on which we rely?

(For a time, years ago, I received Social Security Disability Insurance Survivor Benefits, which were drawn from my deceased mother's Social Security account. This small check is due anyone who had a disability before age twenty-one and relied on a parent who died when the disabled person was still technically a child. There is no savings limit, and the income requirements are reasonable—you can count expenses for an attendant, say, against your earnings, to stay within the parameters. But that program has a strict marriage penalty. You have to remain single. If you marry, you're no longer considered a dependent adult child. When it was discovered that I was receiving the benefit while married, I was cut off *and* told to repay whatever I'd received since marrying. I'm still paying it off today.)

For Laurie and Tim, the cash benefits are just the start. Both of their employers—past and present—provide health insurance that "covers all of our medications," she says, including parts for her bilevel positive airway pressure (BiPAP) machine (which features a mask she wears at night to help her breathe, as many people with SMA and other disorders, including sleep apnea, do), massages, physiotherapy, and even cosmetic Botox. "With respect to my other disability-related stuff, I get a new wheelchair every five or ten years, and my cost-share maximum is five hundred [Canadian] dollars annually. So if I get a power wheelchair, a new wheelchair-seat cushion, and a shower-commode chair in one year, all it will cost me is five hundred dollars."

"Hold on," I say. "We're moving to Canada!"

"It really is pretty easy here," she says.

But later that week, a news item circulates online about a family denied permanent entry into Canada because the son has Down syndrome. The argument is he'd be too costly. That's the downside of a generous benefits program—the backlash, the movement to rein in costs. The authorities can get away with it, apparently, because Canadians with disabilities—who number nearly four million souls, 14 percent of the population—have no basic civil rights protections. It's legal to discriminate on the basis of disability there. So unlike in the United States, there are no mandated ramps, Braille signs, or lift-equipped buses. An initiative to pass an omnibus disability rights law is hopelessly stalled.

When I ask Tim and Laurie if they're sure there isn't anything they'd change about their current situation, they shrug off the idea of disability rights legislation. But they divulge another surprise. Despite their terrific medical benefits, she suffers from chronic and inexplicable pain throughout her body. It's not a symptom of SMA. (SMA affects motor neurons, not sensory nerves.)

I'm left with the feeling that this is a couple with whom I have everything and nothing in common. Our financial situations couldn't be more different, but, like M.L. and me, they've found a connection that works for them—that seems to have satisfied their romantic, financial, and personal-care needs for nearly two decades.

Who could argue with that?

PART III

AGING WITH A DISABILITY, OR WITH A DISABLED PARTNER, AND OTHER JOYS

ALISON AND JOHN

———◆———

FOR A MORE SEASONED perspective on interabled marriage, I catch up with Alison and John Hockenberry. The Hockenberrys have been married for twenty years. Twenty years before that, at the age of nineteen, John severely and permanently injured his spinal cord in a car crash. His injury is an incomplete dural lesion at the T4–T6 level, for those keeping score. It means he's paralyzed from roughly the chest down, which makes him much less disabled—able to manage his own personal-care needs, drive a car with hand controls, and so forth—than some of us.

Yet John is catheter dependent; he's prone to pressure sores called "decubitus ulcers," which can ravage his skin without his even feeling them; and his sexual functioning is inconsistent and undependable, among other limitations. The injury also left him with an incredible drive to succeed, to achieve, to not let his paraplegia limit his options. Five years post-injury he became a correspondent for National Public Radio, where he spent the next dozen years reporting from far-flung war zones, covering the refugees of Desert Storm and other conflicts. He won Peabody Awards and, later, Emmys.

At first he kept his disability a secret. His producers were in Washington, DC, while he was in the Pacific Northwest.

Neither they nor his audience ever saw him. They only heard his golden-throated voice, until the day he couldn't phone in a story on time because the payphone wasn't wheelchair accessible. But by that time he was already an established correspondent. He may have gotten scolded for the delay in filing, but he was not fired. Later, John moved to DC, and everybody at NPR saw his wheelchair up close. When he asked to cover conflicts in Africa and the Middle East, his producers didn't need much convincing.

Minimizing the extent of his disability was as much a self-deception as an attempt to hide his personal life from his bosses and the public. Even later, John continued to trivialize his limitations, as he wrote in his celebrated memoir, *Moving Violations: War Zones, Wheelchairs, and Declarations of Independence*: "It is the rule of this particular game that it be conducted without a word of acknowledgment on my part. To call attention to the wheelchair now by writing about it violates that rule. My mind and soul fight any effort to comment or complain, even now, years after the events I write about."

A change of heart was inevitable.

As his reporting gained attention, John was outed as a paraplegic. Rather than destroying his career, public knowledge of his disability enhanced his reputation. He became widely recognized as the guy who braved bombs and mortar shells from a wheelchair. He moved to TV—NBC and ABC News, in particular—where millions of viewers could see his wheelchair and paraplegic body. As a program host, he was steadfastly apolitical but now fully out of the crip closet.

In 1995, at the age of thirty-nine, two decades after his accident, he seized the moment and put his own spin on events. Not only did he publish his memoir but he then wrote and performed a one-man show in New York, called *Spoke Man*. That's about the time he and Alison, who also worked at ABC News, married.

"We had traveled a lot together for ABC News, worked on a lot of stories," recalls Alison, who is not disabled. Until recently a producer at New York's Documentary Group, a sort of spinoff of ABC News, she's now running the Freakonomics radio and podcast company and has won several Emmy and Peabody awards herself. "We covered a lot of stories together as colleagues."

So before becoming romantically involved with John, she'd seen his disability in action, so to speak, and he didn't try to hide his physical limitations from her. As a result, they were unshackled from some of the awkwardness other interabled couples face.

"I was always very upfront and independent about my physical needs and wanted a limited amount of help, wanted to prove myself as a fully independent partner," John says. But in time, he found that "the inner questions of how being a person with a disability relates to your ability to be honest, to be forthcoming, to be able to ask for help, to be able to express your own needs—that was much more of a challenge."

This observation leads to John Hockenberry's Theory of the Disability Bubble. "The challenges for me have always been related to how the disability puts you in something like a bubble, which makes it harder to communicate, harder to ask for help and do the kinds of things that are really important in a relationship," he says.

I interrupt. John is a rugged man, at least from the waist upward; plus he's a professional journalist and well-known media icon. So I have to steel my self-confidence as I talk with him. "I always thought having a disability meant you were good at asking for help," I say, ever so politely. "It removes artificial barriers of pride and invulnerability."

No dice. I don't think he even considers what I'm saying. Perhaps the difference between us lies in the fact that he experienced disability for the first time as a young adult, whereas my disability is inborn. Or maybe it's a question of degree. He can do more things without help than I can. Either way, I'm no doubt more accustomed to requesting aid than he is. Indeed, I've struggled to teach M.L. how to be clearer about *her* requests—such as which movies she does or doesn't want to see, what she does or doesn't want for dinner, and perhaps especially when she wants company or alone time—this being one of the assets I feel I bring to the marriage. "If you want something to change, why don't you just ask?" I might prompt (hoping it sounds kinder than it might read here).

"In my marriage today," John is saying, "if there are challenges related to the disability, they've been about how being a paraplegic makes you feel like you *can't* ask for help. It makes it hard to talk about what's going on inside of you. It makes you independent to a fault."

Independent to a fault?

"Maybe I could rephrase that," Alison volunteers, leaning in so her shoulder-length fair hair falls forward. "John is very stubbornly independent in terms of proving and demonstrating to himself and others that he can get around just fine, doesn't need help. That's served him well in a lot of ways, and it was appealing and attractive to me. Maybe it's a female thing, to find a very independent, bold person attractive. So those things definitely serve you well in many ways. But in a long-term relationship, communicating about your needs and hearing another person ask you what you need are also important, especially as you age. Being able to be vulnerable and not independent and being able to communicate about that is critical."

She's obviously a strong, independent woman herself. If not for her cooperation, I'm not sure John would've participated in this interview at all. She's curious and sufficiently self-confident to place herself and her husband under my microscope.

In a sense, John was and still is the very definition of a supercrip. During the national struggle for passage of 1990's Americans with Disabilities Act (ADA) and its immediate aftermath, you couldn't help but love the guy. It wasn't his intention to participate in the movement, but once he joined it he became a kind of hero or living example of what the disability rights movement was all about: Empowerment. Integration. Respect. Employability.

This was a mantle he began to wear more comfortably, speaking out and publishing essays about the discrimination he had faced. He became a personal hero of mine.

Alison's introduction to John—the man, not the myth—was from a completely different perspective. Before John, her only experience with disability was interacting with a cousin with Down syndrome. "I didn't know anything about John's disability until I met him in person," she tells me.

If Alison was surprised by any aspect of John's disability—such as his need to self-catheter every few hours or his youthful habit of avoiding all food and drink when on the road to forestall his bathroom needs—and if John was reticent about revealing any of these embarrassing, vulnerable aspects of his disability, neither would acknowledge it to me.

"Alison is my second marriage," John says now. Not long after his release from the hospital, following his accident—while he was still in college—he married a woman he'd met at a rehabilitation facility. "She was in management, and I was a kind of orderly trainer," he recalls. The union didn't last long. "Besides incompatibility and getting married way too early, I was pushed into and out of that relationship because I was insecure about my ability to get around on my own," he reflects.

His deep-seated need to assert his independence undermined his first marriage. It's a tendency he has, in the years since, thought about a lot. With Alison he's tried to temper his machismo, if that's what it is—his inclination to fly solo and remain silent for long periods of time—which has been a coping strategy for counterbalancing his insecurities about being paraplegic, he explains. With Alison he makes a point of being more open.

"As you evolve," says Alison, "and you have the kinds of pressures that John and I have—you know, we have five kids and maintain very demanding jobs—you have to be more open. I think John and I are still learning how to do that well, in a healthy way, even after twenty years. And it's not just John. I have my own issues."

Alison is unabashedly a highly focused, keenly motivated left-brain, type-A personality. Neither she nor John could ever be mistaken for shrinking violets. If they want something done, they go out and do it. Professionally and personally, they are not the type to give up.

And yes, she said five kids.

What turned the collegial friendship between Alison, who was about thirty when they became an item, and John, who is ten years her senior, into a romance? They both pause, then Alison says, "There's something to be said for the fact that I'd spent time with John in pretty extreme environments. We were in conflict zones and remote locations. We were dealing with a lot of primitive infrastructure in the places we traveled together. So I really got to experience—both as a colleague and as a friend—the way he gets around in the world, including in very extreme situations. By the time we became romantically involved, I was already pretty well-versed in how his disability affected or did not affect his ability to get around, and all that meant."

To me, it sounds like something out of Hemingway. But they were not exactly two lost souls buoying each other amid the smoke-filled, blood-soaked ravages of war. They were coprofessionals accustomed to bottling up anxieties and fear in the service of a good story. Neither one was shy or easily shocked.

"All couples have to deal with issues," John quickly adds, which I interpret as an attempt to deflect attention from his disability with a vague generality. That bubble he spoke of is as slippery as Teflon coating. It refracts and repels even a nonhostile gaze. "Has the fact that I'm in a wheelchair gotten in the way physically? No, not really." Pause. "But in terms of being able to communicate, I would say yes."

The very idea of ever being vulnerable or needy felt verboten to him, and maybe to both of them. Since their relationship was to a degree founded on John's strong sense of autonomy, I wonder if the move to greater openness caused shockwaves.

"No," Alison responds. "The surprising thing maybe is just how difficult it's been to learn how to communicate about vulnerability, to try to understand where each other is coming from on this issue. John had twenty years of pretty significant experiences that'd shaped how he lived his life, and I wasn't there for that. Those were pretty well-honed coping mechanisms for approaching life."

It makes sense. When couples tie the knot, they have to learn how to live together, which entails more than remembering to put down the toilet seat or replace the cap on the toothpaste tube or put knives into the dishwasher point-side down or insert the toilet paper so that it unrolls in the right direction . . . Come to think of it, there are a million aspects to marital behavior modification. Not to mention accommodating bad moods and the mutual need for occasional privacy.

With disability, I think now, the adjustments can be even more involved. Many crips, for instance, have a lot of equipment they need to fit into the bedroom, and unless you have a lot of space, that'll easily fill more than half the room. What's more, some people with disabilities require a particular type of bed. Many of us take several hours just to get up and dressed in the morning. Some have dietary restrictions. If we have personal-care assistants, there's a whole additional personality to fit into the home space. And for me, there are organizational aspects too. Like a blind person who needs to know exactly where everything is, I've had to insist on a fairly rigid system because of my physical limitations. It's partly because I rely on different attendants. You need consistency when you have different people helping you. But also, with an off-kilter anatomy like mine, you have to schedule meals and bathroom breaks and know in advance which position will cause unbearable pressure-pain in the next three hours. Spontaneity gets leached out, and rigorous self-discipline drilled in.

I wonder aloud if John has experienced that. Since he's had to schedule his food intake and bathroom breaks to accommodate a busy schedule and unfriendly or inaccessible terrain, I'm sure he knows exactly what I mean about self-discipline, about being strict with yourself. But how does that square with being a family man? How do you loosen the reins to accommodate often-chaotic family dynamics?

"Some of the qualities that work really, really well as an independent journalist who is also someone with a disability are not the kinds of things you need to be a good parent," he allows. "I mean, you need to be able to answer kids' wide-open questions about what's going on with you. You need to be able to say to your son or daughter, maybe four times a day, why you can't walk. Or what happened to make you break your back. And you have to be able to do that and not be tired of it. You have to really understand how the child is learning how you're different from other people and how that's okay. You can't be like, 'Hey, I'm fine. Don't notice me. I'm not just a wheelchair.' You know? That doesn't work with your kids."

Kids. *Five* kids. I ask about this next, about their decision to have children, which I find rare among interabled couples.

For the Hockenberrys, it had to be a conscious decision because their pregnancy required in vitro fertilization (although not for their youngest child). "Poor sperm quality is a very common corollary to paraplegia, and then there was an unpredictability in his sexual functioning," says Alison, adding, "although it all apparently worked with perfect, unplanned timing to produce our surprise fifth child."

Survivors of spinal-cord injury tend to have fertility issues. A great deal of research has been done to help paraplegic men achieve erections (less, I'm told with some disdain, to help paraplegic women regain genital pleasure). Artificially induced ejaculation is possible. The results can then be inserted into the womb. With IVF, egg production is also artificially stimulated to maximize the chances of fertilization, hence the frequency of IVF twins. While this process is not uncommon these days, it is also not a process couples begin thoughtlessly or heedlessly. For one thing, it's expensive. For another, it's emotionally grueling.

"The decision to become parents, that was a hard road," acknowledges John. "Alison really drove that effort. I was more passive about it. I think I had a real fear of failure. It was a tangible fear. I feared it wouldn't work. I feared we'd have to adopt. I feared having to go through the adoption process, where I might have to prove I'd be a good parent, and I really didn't want to be in that situation."

As adoptive or foster parents, people with disabilities can be put under more rigorous scrutiny than the able-bodied. In 2012 the National Council on Disability reported widespread "bias and unnecessary barriers to foster care and adoption placements based on speculation and stereotypes" about disabled adults' parenting skills. In 2015 the US Justice Department and Department of Health and Human Services issued joint guidelines to put an end to such barriers, noting there had been "an increasing number of discrimination complaints" by prospective parents with disabilities. It's illegal; the ADA is supposed to protect parents with disabilities from discrimination in all child-welfare programs and services. Yet discrimination is rampant. What's more, those who seek to adopt internationally may find outright bans against them by foreign countries for which there is no redress.

This is what John feared. After all, he wasn't used to being found lacking. He wasn't used to being excluded from anything. And he certainly wasn't used to failure.

"When Alison got pregnant—and we had twins right off the bat—that's when I joined the party completely. It was remarkable how little I'd thought about it. I mean, I [knew] kids were important to me, but it wasn't until I got together with Alison that I truly understood I had a lot more thinking left to do. I had to get up to speed quickly once Alison got pregnant. It was surprising how prepared I was for things *not* to work out, but Alison was on the other side of the spectrum. She was totally determined that it *was* going to work out. And she was right. Everything worked out really well."

We smile, all three of us, thinking about our children.

Later, I reverse course and ask about John's career. "John," I begin slowly, "I'm wondering if you started in radio partly to hide your disability."

"Radio and TV weren't significantly different," he replies quickly. Yet he has to admit that being invisible might've helped early on. "The only real issue of disability in my career is the fact that, because I was in radio and I was working as a freelancer, the people I was filing stories for didn't know I was disabled. By the time they found out, I'd already done a million stories, so they realized I could handle it."

He categorically denies ever feeling discriminated against by the networks. There were questions about whether his wheelchair should be shown on TV, but they were more a matter of aesthetics than prejudice.

"The issues I faced were no different from what any other correspondent faces," he insists.

Yet there was a hint of prejudice from an in-law, says Alison. "My uncle, who is a priest, said to me at the very beginning, when I first told him [about John], 'You know, sometimes people who get involved with people with a disability tend to have a need to be helpful.' He thought that was something I should think about. And then he read John's memoir, which came out the same summer that we got engaged, and within a month he sent me an e-mail that basically said, 'Never mind. He doesn't seem like somebody who needs a whole lot of help.' So I think it was a little eye-opening for my uncle just to read John's book and get a more educated perspective on what kind of life a person in a wheelchair might be living. Aside from that, I don't remember anybody saying anything like, 'Are you sure you want to marry a guy in a wheelchair?' But that said, most of our friends were people who also worked with John, who'd also seen him traipsing around war zones and stuff."

John adds, "Probably everybody knew if they did question my worthiness to marry, I would come back at them so forcefully . . ."

I push further. What about when he and Alison are out in public together? Is John so famous that no one treats him like an incompetent imbecile in public? In restaurants, no waiter asks Alison what "he" will be having?

"It *was* an issue for us how other people saw us together," says John. "People would only talk to Alison; they wouldn't talk to me. Or they'd conclude something about us. This was only an issue early on, I think, because, before Alison, I'd learned to tune out this sort of thing. I was less conscious of people looking at me. But Alison was suddenly very conscious of being the center of attention when we were a couple."

"And that was uncomfortable?" I prompt.

"The only thing I can compare it to is being an interracial couple," he says tersely.

But these uncomfortable encounters only made them feel closer.

"It really pushes you together," John continues. "The way you're looked at externally can produce anxiety, and you need to talk about that together as a couple. It sort of makes you be honest. And then, as time goes on, you need to make sure you're aware of how different you are from each other. One person is disabled, the other is not. You need to make sure you're really communicating at the deepest level, and sometimes disability can get in the way—particularly the idea that 'I've got everything figured out' and that kind of stuff. It can be a real hindrance. So you have to burst that bubble."

Of course, I point out, a lot of men go through a version of that: the independent, macho attitude.

John agrees, but only so far. "It probably mirrors that, to a certain extent," he clarifies. He then wonders aloud whether spinal-cord injured women react differently to their injuries than spinal-cord injured men do to theirs. Do women become as single-minded about preserving their autonomy? Do they have to work as hard at loosening up and trusting others? He's talking, I think, about the fact that women may be more willing to work together with other people, that they're less likely to need to assert their dominance or feel as threatened by a collective effort than many men. On the other hand, men may be more comfortable with giving instructions, being assertive in explaining how someone should lift a wheelchair over steps, for instance. Or maybe it comes down to how we and society define ourselves: Does a man have to be strong and autonomous to feel like a man? Does a woman have to be graceful and giving to feel like a woman? And does disability make us any less male or female than we naturally are? "There are certain gender issues that work really well for a male with a spinal-cord injury and not so well for a female and vice versa," he muses.

This is touchy territory. It occurs to me that perhaps he and Alison don't know other interabled couples, or at least not well enough to have this kind of discussion with them. I ask about how things are with their peers.

"If anything," says John, "people typically err on the side of thinking we're Super Parents, which we're not. They seem to think we're amazing, while we're very conscious of the fact that we're just trying to keep our heads above water."

He laughs. It's the oldest complaint in the disability world: we're either pitied or put on a pedestal. Every disabled person I know gets told by nondisabled friends and colleagues that he or she is amazing or inspirational. But it's the first time John's admitted to me that there *is* an occasional discrepancy between how he feels and how he's perceived. Then he allows another.

"Sometimes if I'm out with my kids and Alison isn't around, people will presume they're not mine. Sometimes they think I'm their grandfather."

I ask how he handles such encounters.

"If somebody calls me out, if somebody says, 'Hey, you're out with Grandpa, huh?' to my five-year-old, it's like, *Thanks for making my day*. For me it's more a matter of my age," says the then fifty-eight-year-old, "than my disability. Though early on, when our first twins were infants, there might've been a time when somebody said, 'Watch out for that man'—thinking I was just some random person in a wheelchair who was going to roll over these kids, not their father, not completely in control of the situation. That wasn't fun, that experience. But it's only a moment, and it passes. There aren't many like that."

This issue, how to react to such nuisances, has come up so often in M.L.'s and my life and in the lives of other interabled couples! I ask the Hockenberrys, "Do you find that sometimes your tolerance levels for these kinds of things varies—or are you two always in agreement about how to react?"

A short pause ensues. "Sometimes," Alison starts, "it's just your mood that determines how tolerant you feel."

The answer is diplomatically put but unsatisfying. I guess I've been searching for some source of discord between them. Can they really be such an in-sync couple?

I know our time together is running out. The Hockenberrys are on a strict schedule. But I can't help thinking they've left something out, some regret or frustration. "If you could change one thing about your situation, what would it be?" I ask. "More outside help, more privacy, a cure for paraplegia?"

"More babysitting help," Alison answers promptly. "More household help in general, so we could have more time together. We're just so busy!" She concedes they're fortunate. They do have some hired help. "But parenting is very, very challenging," she says, doubtless echoing parents everywhere. "I can't think of anything related to the disability issues, though. Right, John?"

"Right," he agrees. "I know one thing—we'd love to be billionaires!" A round of polite chuckles ensues. He goes on to say that even with billions of dollars he wouldn't have a hired cook.

"We've got a kitchen that's universally designed and set up so it's easy for John to cook," Alison explains. "It's also easy for the kids to cook, ever since they were little, because we have these low prep tables where you can chop and roll stuff out and prepare the meals."

When kitchen counters—and, for that matter, light switches and radio controls and bookshelves and just about everything else—are low enough for a person in a wheelchair to reach, they're also accessible to small children. For better or worse. I recall my kids' blasting the stereo when they were three and four years old, startling themselves as well as their parents—a reaction they liked, and liked repeating!

"There are things like that in our lives," says Alison, referring to their accessible kitchen, "that we're fortunate to have, and [they] make the disability issues sort of melt away." She stammers for a moment, unsure if what she'd said was appropriate. "Right, Hon?"

"And they allow us to cook together," John adds, "which becomes a sort of shared family adventure."

"Yes," says Alison. They are again in sync.

"So there's really not a lot of disability-related stress in your lives?"

"Well, I do worry about the future," Alison slips in. "I worry about when our kids are out of the house and it's just John and me. John is ten years older than I am. It's not like we haven't been honest with ourselves about that, but we haven't really had time to sit down and talk about how that's going to work, what the issues will be. Right now we don't have a lot of disability-related anxiety. That's an anxiety for the future."

Aging with a disability—for some, it's a double whammy of debility. "I've been sensing Alison's anxiety," says John. "I'm very conscious of wanting to be around as the kids grow up, and that's given me a whole new level of discipline about maintaining my own health. I very much want to be in this for the long game." He's quite serious; I can tell by his tone of voice, the quickening of his breath. "I'm extremely conscious of my weight. Extremely conscious about exercise and diet," he continues, sounding much like any other educated, self-aware middle-aged man. But then he ventures a disability-specific spin: "I'm also very conscious about my skin integrity."

He's talking about those pressure sores or decubitus ulcers, which are common for those who sit still all day long. John has to lift himself up off his butt periodically, change positions to minimize undue pressure and moisture buildup. Fortunately, he has the arm strength to do that. He just has to remember to do it and to avoid pressing too long on one spot to ease the pressure on another. Positional shifts have to be constant. If he fails, if a pressure wound or skin sore begins to develop, he has to stay off his chair until it heals, which can take weeks or even months if it's bad. A bad sore gone untreated can become a dangerous infection. The same degree of care is necessary for his catheter routine. Urinary tract infections are common among para- and quadriplegics. At the same time, many need manual assistance to empty their bowels completely—literal shit shovelers.

"I do not screw up at all," he is saying now. "There is zero tolerance for bad behavior. Which was not always the case for me."

When he was younger, partly in denial about his vulnerability, perhaps in pursuit of a difficult story, he would often deny his bodily needs or put off tending to them as long as possible, as when he'd avoid drinking water so he wouldn't have to whip out a catheter in the middle of the Iraqi desert. But age can decrease physical stamina. The body becomes less patient, less malleable and resilient. This reminds me of a passage from his book: "My entire existence had become a mission of never saying no to the physical challenges the world presented to a wheelchair. It was this that had gotten me through a fiery accident and would provide me with a mission upon which I could hang the rest of my life."

Since then, he's learned: it can be better to say no to physical challenges. Safer, healthier, smarter.

To wrap up, I ask bluntly, "What do you think of my assertion that disability can get couples to maintain an enviable degree of honesty, mutual sharing, and give-and-take? Does that sound right, or am I stretching the point?"

There's a long silence, and I fear I haven't expressed myself adequately.

"I see what you mean," John says, mercifully. "I do wonder about that. Early on, my disability might've put us in touch with issues of our physical selves that other couples take longer to come around to. You have to be conscious of physical issues that many other couples don't really need to be. So I do think that was a help to us."

It's gratifying to hear John say that he finds it helpful—the ability to be "in touch," as he puts it, to share a closeness that other couples have to work harder or longer to achieve. It's gratifying because I agree wholeheartedly.

DORENE AND STEVE

———◆———

M.L. IS FEEDING ME DINNER, skillfully maneuvering a forkful of rotisserie chicken into my eager but tight-jawed mouth. I try to facilitate with my tongue and lips, but there's a problem. "Too big," I manage to say, despite my overwhelmed mandibles.

"It's tiny."

"Not to me," I say, spitting some into my napkin.

It looks rude, and I wouldn't do it in public. But I don't want to gag or choke. M.L. knows this. She understands that I require baby-sized bites because of my swallowing difficulties, though sometimes she forgets just how small or gets a little adventurous. To be honest, some days I'm pickier than others.

I also know that she feeds me better than anyone else. If I had to rely on friends, family, and paid people to feed me all the time, instead of just at breakfast and lunch, I'd be even skinnier than I am. With other feeders, so much food ends up on my shirt I sometimes just want to give up. The two years that M.L. did all my feeding, when the girls were infants and we had to let all the hired help go so we could afford to have M.L. stay home with them, were my fattest—in a good, healthy way. Ever since, keeping weight on has become a problem for me.

After talking to Alison and John, who plainly function well apart from each other, and Laurie and Tim, who seem to prefer to be as involved in each other's lives as possible, I'm thinking a lot about how I meet my nutritional needs. In eating as in all other aspects of life, I like to believe I could manage fine on my own, if I had to rely solely on paid help, say. But honestly, I'm not 100 percent sure. I used to cope without M.L., of course, but that was decades ago. We've been together so long, it's hard to know anymore how either of us would manage solo. Looking back, there's no doubt M.L. aided my escape from parental control, but that doesn't mean I wouldn't have flown free otherwise, does it? That's not why I fell for her. I can't deny M.L. is a natural-born helper. She worked as a nanny in college and became an elementary school teacher not just because she likes kids; she also likes being of service. She's the sort of person who will go out of her way to inform a stranger of an untied shoelace. But is that the reason we're together and have stayed together—because I need so much physical help and she needs to be helpful?

M.L. says no and that I should stop fishing for compliments. But to settle my troubled mind, I set out to gain a fresh perspective from another long-lasting interabled couple. And I can think of few better examples than my old friend Dorene Giacopini and her husband, Steve Wilson. Dorene and I were at Harvard together, in Quincy House, the dorm for upperclassmen (and upperclasswomen) where the esteemed university put its physically disabled students in those days. Dorene was born with spina bifida.

"I learned to walk on crutches when I was two," she tells me in our first phone interview. Occurring in one of two thousand births in the United States (more often in other countries), spina bifida involves a malformation of the spine in utero—specifically, the tubing that normally encases the spine fails to close. Resulting symptoms vary from weak limbs, paralysis, and/or seizures to, most severely, hydrocephalus, which is usually deadly.

At fifty-six, Dorene is a muscular woman, no doubt from hauling herself around on crutches much of the time. Her body does not appear atrophied or skeletal, and her physique isn't twisted in any discernible way, except for her legs, which hang down like floppy marionettes. I don't think I've ever seen her wearing shoes, just thick socks.

What made her really stand out in our Cambridge days was her laid-back California attitude. "You Northeasterners are so uptight," she'd tease between bites of Greek salad in the echoey dining hall. "Chill *out!*"

After Harvard, she graduated from the University of California, Berkeley, School of Law. From there, she worked for her congressman, Norman Mineta (later US secretary of transportation), "during ADA negotiations," she says in a subsequent conversation. A series of positions related to special education, as an attorney and mediator, followed. For the past twenty years she's also served on the Bay Area's Metropolitan Transportation Commission as a representative of the US Department of Transportation. She's a director of the Disability Rights Education and Defense Fund and current president of the Board of Community Resources for Independent Living.

We last saw each other a couple of years ago, when she visited LA. I was taken aback to see her now in a wheelchair; it's become her primary mode of locomotion, she informed me. The surprising thing was, she actually looked better—healthier, hardier, stronger, more serene—on wheels than she had on sticks. Nearly thirty years had passed, and she almost seemed younger.

Six years after her graduation—two years ahead of mine—Dorene became romantically linked with Steve, a mild-mannered Yalie. "We actually first met, without really meeting, at a Harvard–Yale [football] game," she's telling me now. "I slept on the floor of his living room in New Haven." I can see she's still a teaser. Met without meeting?

"If so, we didn't really interact in any significant way then," Steve puts in. He's a soft-spoken man with a mid-length gray beard, round glasses, and a charming grin. A good match for Dorene's smiling face, on which the expression is still as fun-loving and warm as a fresh-from-the-oven muffin. "We *really* met sometime later," he continues, "when Dorene gave me a ride to a [mutual] friend's wedding reception. We ended up having dinner together [that night] and became friends. I was in another relationship at the time."

Dorene could give him a ride because she's able to drive—originally by adjusting the pedals, and then, after age fifty, with hand controls. She was always pretty quick and agile on her crutches, I recall. She never had much trouble getting around Harvard's ancient, sprawling, cobblestoned campus (which sure as hell wasn't the case for me!) or traveling to and from the West Coast. It doesn't surprise me that she'd travel to New Haven for a football game or sleep on a stranger's floor or agree to a friend's request to give a stranger a ride in her car. But to look at her, these things might surprise you. Her disability is anything but invisible.

"How familiar were you with spina bifida or people with disabilities in general before Dorene?" I ask Steve.

"Not at all, really."

"You did have a condition that caused you to use crutches for a little bit in high school, right?" Dorene intercedes.

He clears his throat. "Yes, for a very short time. I had a little early onset arthritis and used crutches for about six months. But that's it."

I like the mellifluous, gentle timbre of his voice. He uses no-drama phrases like "very short time" and "a little early onset." Perhaps he minimizes where she enlarges.

After Yale, Steve earned a PhD in linguistics at UC Berkeley, and while there he coached a high school debating team for extra money. He found he loved working with that age group and now teaches high school history and linguistics. It sounds like the perfect job for him. What's more, listening to Dorene and Steve, I'm convinced they communicate well and respect each other's feelings and perspectives.

I find it curious, though, that she makes a point of drawing on a shared experience—crutches—that he seems to feel isn't relevant or noteworthy. I delve more deeply into their early days together.

The dinner they had together after Dorene gave Steve that fateful ride to a friend's wedding reception was in 1987, when they were both twenty-seven years old. "We continued to see each other off and on for another year, as friends," says Steve, "and then, when my other relationship ended, we started seeing each other more seriously."

I detect a furtive smile.

"We've been together ever since," he goes on. "We didn't end up moving in together till '91. In '93 we got a dog. Two years later we bought a house. And in 1998 we got married! That's the timeline, the résumé of our relationship. And yes, we did things a little out of the traditional order."

"A little." No-drama Steve. I ask if there's a particular significance to this timeline, and they both shrug. So I ask about reactions to their union from friends and family. This time it's like striking gold—valuable if you sift through the crumbs.

"My mother had some concerns . . . " Steve begins.

"Your mother," says Dorene, "was concerned about whether I'd develop hydrocephalus."

"Yes, she had some medical knowledge, which gave her some medical concerns," Steve concurs. His mother was a neonatal nurse and had seen babies with spina bifida. "She was also concerned about your life expectancy. But my mother was a complicated figure. I think she was in some ways a *little* conventional. She had reservations about our relationship. But in the end, she was supportive of our marriage. She was even part of our wedding and all that."

He's putting things gingerly, yet he and Dorene seem resolved about the past, seem to bear no grudges or hard feelings. I infer that wasn't always so, though, given the slow pace of their relationship and the nontraditional order in which they crept up on marriage. (Separately, Dorene tells me *he* was the shy one; she'd been waiting for a proposal for years!) "At the time, did you have a particular strategy in mind for coping with family reactions?" I ask.

There's a long quiet moment, and I wonder which one is going to answer first. Steve breaks the silence. "When I told my mother I was dating Dorene, before they'd met in person, I said, 'She uses crutches and has spina bifida.' My mother's reaction was something along the lines of, 'Oh.' She'd occasionally have questions about Dorene, but if she held deeper concerns, she definitely didn't express them. Not directly anyway."

Of course, Steve didn't exactly invite further comment either. He set a tone of breezy matter-of-factness with his mother. He was informative, didn't hide anything about Dorene's disability, but delivered the news with a neutrality worthy of a TV anchor.

It wasn't long before Steve's mother met Dorene. The couple drove down to Steve's mother's place in LA. Sometimes putting a human face on a diagnosis can turn anxiety into acceptance—especially if the face is attached to someone as friendly and dynamic as Dorene. The meeting went fine. But acceptance became a moot point when Steve's mother developed her own medical problems, which led to her early retirement and, eventually, her death.

"That was a counterbalancing issue," says Steve, "because she was spending a lot of time on her own health concerns."

Dorene's parents, on the other hand, had a completely different reaction about her marriage to Steve.

"My folks were fine with Steve, pretty much," she says. "The only thing that was really weird was, after we got the dog and the house and everything, we got engaged . . . and *that's* when they were shocked. Absolutely shocked! My mom can be very opinionated. She tells you what she wants to tell you. But my dad, who was a nice guy, even *he* was uncharacteristically flabbergasted."

I'm not getting it. I ask, "What was so flabbergasting?"

"If I had to bet," says Dorene, "I'd wager they thought I'd never get married. My mother had told me as much in the past."

She adds they also might have been concerned about the financial implications of her marriage to Steve—something related to how her parents had structured their estate plans. "Not sure, but it was definitely a weird reaction. My parents' assumption was that no sane male would want to marry a woman with spina bifida. And maybe they were right!"

Like me, Dorene was always sent to regular schools, not separated from able-bodied students, which was unusual in the 1960s. "Mom had very high expectations for me academically but never taught me how to do anything practical," says Dorene. "She was, in my humble opinion, traumatized by having to be the primary care-giver of a kid with a disability when she would've been perfectly happy to continue working and going out every weekend. For her, it just always seemed easier to do things herself than teach me how to do them. As a result, I was woefully underprepared to live on my own."

Sounds like a mixed message, I prompt. Young Dorene was told to get an education and to have fun, but she wasn't expected to grow into a normal independent adult. I ask her again to help me understand.

"Mom told me I wouldn't be getting married so I needed a good job that would take care of me financially and provide satis-faction," Dorene explains. "Even when I was in high school, Mom was involved with a group of parents of mostly intellectually dis-abled kids, [a group] that was trying to build housing for us since we wouldn't ever be able to live alone."

"Forgive me," I interrupt, "but you were physically able to do so much for yourself, why was she sure you wouldn't be able to live independently?"

"My parents were working-class, Ben. They had no concept of having service providers help with anything at home. If I couldn't do everything, I could do nothing."

Like me, she has beaten the odds. Or at least the odds her mother laid. "So they were overprotective?" I say.

She laughs. "Hell no! Mom didn't think she had to worry about me getting 'in trouble' because sex wasn't even in the cards, she felt." That's not what I meant, exactly, I start to say—not *that* kind of protection. I'm silent, though, to let Dorene go on. "She pretty much let me do whatever the hell I wanted. No curfews. She wanted me to have fun while I still could, before everyone else paired off and I was alone."

Alone? Dorene? Sounds impossible, unthinkable. She's so extroverted. I come back with this: "To me, you've always come across as brave and outgoing. Is that because of the freedoms you had as a teenager, do you think? Or is that just bluster, your sociability? Just a put-on?"

Her dad, she explains, was an extreme extrovert, and it's a trait she inherited.

I can't help but admire how Dorene and Steve appear to approach even awkward situations such as meeting each other's parents with grace and good humor. That kind of casual self-confidence, I think, can only come after you've wrestled with some gnarly obstacles. Wrestled and won.

The next time we talk, I ask about their personal-assistance needs. I know Dorene gets around by herself with seeming ease, but what really goes on at home? I'm trying to get a sense of how much she depends on Steve, and vice versa, when no one is looking.

"Sometimes I need Steve to help me put my shoes on," she answers.

That stops me in my tracks. Shoes? Is that symbolic of, well, getting dressed and a whole lot more? A beat passes. "Okay," I say. "And what else?"

"And he does most of the stuff around the house. He kind of helps me in and out of difficulties. I need Steve to help me out of difficulties more than before. And he's doing more and more around the house. We have a housekeeper and gardener every two weeks, but still—"

"That sounds like it could be serious. What kinds of difficulties?"

"Little things."

I go for a few specific examples. "But you're able to drive yourself places, get yourself to the bathroom, and so forth?"

"Yes."

Okay, she can do all that—but not the laundry and vacuuming? Or does Steve just like doing household chores? Have they instituted this division of labor for a particular reason—such as to upend traditional gender roles? Before I can formulate the question, Steve joins the conversation.

"Dorene has told me that she was told over and over again as a child, 'Don't worry about [doing] that. Don't even try. Let me get it for you.' As a result, I sometimes think she doesn't attempt tasks she could do just because she's used to having other people do them. Laundry and things like that."

I check to make sure Dorene isn't offended. She says, "Mmmm," and nods in agreement. They are nothing if not a peaceful pair.

"Not like it's a big deal," Steve continues, perhaps aware that he might've sounded harsh. "But occasionally I'll ask her to do something or suggest, 'You know you *can* do this if you need to.'" The term "learned helplessness" leaps to my mind. It doesn't sound as though Steve resents Dorene's inability or unwillingness to do these things, even if the implication is that Dorene is needlessly dependent or even lazy.

"Mostly it's just a matter of habits we're in—we're *both* in," he goes on. "We get used to things done a certain way. In an ideal world, I suppose we should get out of our ruts a little bit, in terms of what types of stuff we do."

It sounds like an Aha Moment in couples therapy: *Switch up the routine. Trade places around household chores.* Then again, those of us of a certain age do tend to get stuck in old habits. I make a mental note not to assume this is a disability issue per se. But the next thing Dorene says forces me to reconsider.

"He's right," she says, as unfailingly amiable as ever. "But honestly, I'd be more inclined to do laundry if there were enough maneuvering space in the laundry room to turn my wheelchair around. I'd be more inclined to cook if we would finally get around to remodeling our kitchen to make it more accessible." For a brief moment I wonder if she's playing the crip card or even feeling defensive. But neither approach would be in character for her.

What she says next, however, *is* in character: "There's no reason we haven't made those things more accessible other than the fact that I can't get out of my own way to do them."

"That's the larger answer," Steve puts in. "It would be good to have a lifestyle that's better adapted to our current practical needs, to make household activities more doable. If, you know, we ever get around to it."

I note the operative word "current," which suggests that Dorene's limitations have changed, increased. The wheelchair is the most obvious sign. It's not uncommon for disabilities to worsen with age, of course. I know all about that. My SMA keeps progressing at its petty pace. My hands are significantly weaker than they were fifteen years ago. I fully expect to become ventilator-dependent before I'm sixty. Declining health isn't the exclusive privilege of the disabled, to be sure. M.L. herself has the normal aches and pains of middle age. She watches her cholesterol and carbs. She finds certain things she used to do with relative ease have become too difficult. But somehow when your daily life activities have already been circumscribed by disability, each new incremental restriction can feel frighteningly unjust.

Yet Dorene doesn't appear to feel sorry for herself at all. It was an ordinary random morning five years ago, she tells me, when she got up to go to the bathroom and found she "just couldn't walk as usual." She was fifty-one. "Never got better. I spent years trying to figure it out."

Her doctors, in their infinite wisdom, concluded she was simply getting older.

"Dorene has gone from using crutches most of the time and only occasionally using a chair to always using a chair and using crutches only for transitions—that's the number one practical change in our lives," says Steve. Nary a shred of dismay or resentment comes through his voice. "It's required different kinds of adaptations—more use of ramps and things."

They've mostly adjusted to it by now. "It's not all bad," Dorene adds. "Since I've been using a wheelchair, all of a sudden I have hands! I can do things I couldn't before, like pace around while talking on the phone, which I used to watch other people do with envy." *Pace*, as in drive one's wheelchair back and forth across the room. I do it myself sometimes. "I can move objects around much more easily now. I can walk the dog, carry groceries without dangling a grocery bag from a finger that's also holding a crutch," she says. "I still couldn't do these things from a manual wheelchair, but with a power chair I can hold and carry a lot. . . . So in a way, I feel like I have more functionality than before."

Now that she's using a wheelchair full-time, she also has to exercise three times a week to make up for the workout she used to get by hauling herself around on crutches. "In many ways I'm healthier than ever. I was getting lots of headaches from the way I walked, which disappeared when I started using the chair."

Healthier than ever, and it shows, I'm thinking. But now I ask the terrible question: does she know what the state of her disability may be in another five or ten years?

"I have longevity on both sides of my family," she answers (as I write this, her mother just turned one hundred). "I'm in the first generation of people with spina bifida—who needed spine closure at birth—to survive, so they have very little info to give me." In fact, she says, medical professionals "just like to study me."

"I know the feeling," I say. "I've been a human guinea pig most of my life. Folks like us weren't supposed to survive."

There's another complication for Dorene and Steve related to her wheelchair use: it makes traveling more difficult—especially by air. Way back in 1990, the airlines somehow got an exemption from the ADA. (Instead, they are subject to the far less stringent Air Carriers Access Act.) So wheelchairs still cannot be rolled onto airplanes of any size, and wheelchair-using passengers are required to transfer to a regular plane seat. Unless the wheelchair can be disassembled or collapsed to fit within an onboard closet—which power wheelchairs never can—it will be swiped away and stowed with baggage (and inevitably damaged). And, needless to say, airplane bathrooms are far too minuscule to be accessible.

Air travel remains one of the last frontiers for disability rights activists. A Chicago-based nonprofit called Open Doors Organization has been fighting to improve access to all manner of travel and tourism since 2000. In its 2015 survey, it found that eleven million travelers with disabilities took twenty-three million trips over the preceding two years and spent a total of $9 billion on flights. Yes, that means some crips *are* managing to travel. But fully 72 percent of those air travelers complained of "major obstacles." In early 2016, the Department of Transportation was said to be exploring the possibility of revamping air accommodations, but there's no word yet as to when or in what ways that might happen.

"Traveling is definitely something I'd like to do more—and my change in disability has affected this," Dorene says. "If I do travel, especially internationally, I need more help from Steve—and he's really a homebody, which is why I used to travel a lot on my own. So using a chair is definitely cramping my style in terms of travel."

I bring Steve back into the discussion and ask about his ability to cope with Dorene's increased limitations, his energy levels, and any age-related limitations of his own. "As far as my aging goes, other than the fact that I can't remember anything"—he chuckles—"no, there's nothing. Except that if we're traveling, we now have to take a travel scooter, one I can lift up and put in trunks of cars. So things like that have become more . . . complicated."

"There is one thing," Dorene interjects. "This may have nothing to do with my disability—it probably has more to do with how busy Steve has become at work. But he's gotten much more efficient about getting household stuff done. He takes the initiative to start projects and completes them on his own. Before, I often felt like I was the one who would initiate the big projects." She pauses. They are a considerate couple, considerate of each other. "Does that ring true with you?" she asks him.

"Not sure. I certainly don't feel like I've been more proactive because your abilities have narrowed, or anything like that."

Later that day, for the thousandth time, I sign an online petition to compel airlines to make their vehicles as accessible as most city buses.

"What do you make of Dorene's political activism, Steve?" I ask later. "Are you involved too?"

Dorene is a disability rights activist of the best kind: effective, logical, but never abrasive or strident. That's how the former mediator was trained. I'm wondering if disability advocacy has been a unifying or a divisive issue between them. In the BC years (before children), I was involved with the movement too. Actually, it was M.L. who first got excited about the issues, after reading about them in the *Disability Rag*, the seminal advocacy newsletter of the 1980s. I wasn't political and I wasn't a joiner, until I faced seemingly endless job discrimination—which, given my Harvard pedigree, I could only attribute to disability prejudice.

I went to protest demonstrations, volunteered at my local independent-living center, and wrote speeches and op-ed essays in support of the cause. M.L. would drive me to and from meetings, if necessary—and even attended the occasional activist event—but she is inherently nonconfrontational. Besides, as an able-bodied person (or "TABby," as some say, for Temporarily Able-Bodied), she felt somewhat out of place. The able-bodied were sort of considered the enemies, after all.

To this day M.L. and I occasionally argue about aspects of the cause. I feel she's too comfortable with the status quo, but I also know that she helps keep me grounded in reality. For instance, I'm sure she's right that not everybody hates, fears, or pities every crip they encounter. Not anymore, anyway. Many people have learned to accept and even respect us. But, I'll tell her, I just want to make sure it stays that way.

"I certainly try to support Dorene's efforts," Steve is saying. He chooses his words carefully, diplomatically. "In some cases I do feel like an outsider in some of those situations, but I'm supportive of all the causes she endorses."

He goes on to explain that "one of the defining things" about their relationship is that she's an extrovert and he's an introvert. "Many of these kinds of involvement things would never occur to me," he says. "I'll sit at home and write a check, but going out and doing the political side of something is really not me at all. I'm kind of like 'the good wife,' you know? The type who'll stand there beside her but not be proactively involved in any of it."

I imagine that must lead to fights sometimes, but no animosity is evident today. Maybe they're just on "interview behavior." But I like the way they appear to manage the separate/together stuff. Though she's needing more physical assistance as she ages, that doesn't seem to impede either partner's sense of autonomy.

It's a warm February day when I get to chat with Dorene again. This time she appears sans Steve. I ask the big question: Why no children?

"Steve never wanted to have kids," she says, betraying zero regret. "I never really wanted to either. Thought about it seriously for a while, when I turned thirty-five. He was willing, but I don't think either of us wanted to be a primary caretaker."

I'm wondering if her disability played a role in that. Did they choose not to have children because they couldn't cope with one more thing—one more needy, not fully independent person in the household?

"Even at my most interested point," says Dorene, "I wasn't interested enough in raising a kid to do it with someone who wasn't totally into it." She also allows that she didn't want to be like her mother, who she's convinced resented the time and energy that parenting took.

"What were those conversations like, between you two?" I pry.

"Like a lot of our conversations," she says. "He generally doesn't like to rock the boat but is willing to do stuff if I want to."

It strikes me once again that the way couples negotiate their differences and shared responsibilities has more to do with their personalities and individual strengths and weaknesses than any disability either one might have. Marriage is marriage, as varied and delicately balanced as it can be, and the presence of a disability is just one part of it. Interabled marriage is not an exception to the pattern; a disability doesn't alter the underlying formula.

I conclude with my standard final question: If Dorene could change one thing about her and Steve's current situation, what would it be? More help? More money? Better health?

"An ocean view," she says.

I laugh a long time, but for an instant I fear I've asked an offensively simplistic question. She throws me a lifeline.

"But seriously," Dorene continues, "hired help *would* be cool. I would have no problem having a personal valet—somebody to hold things when I'm getting dressed and that kind of stuff. I mean, I watch *Downton Abbey*."

I chuckle again. It's a pleasant image: personal-care assistant as valet. I've always wondered why some people refer to PCAs as nurses when I've always preferred to see mine as butlers, chauffeurs, bodyguards, or gentlemen's gentlemen. Everything is what you make it.

GLORIA AND SEBASTIAN

———◆———

AS I REACH OUT TO INTERABLED COUPLES, I begin to fear hearing the same rhythms and refrains over and over again. Everyone is totally in love. All of them accept their partners completely. Everyone believes in honesty and humility and helpfulness.

Then I meet an unassuming couple who surprises me. Here is their story.

About a half hour south of San Francisco, at the southern end of Silicon Valley, is a pretty bedroom community I'll call Dobson Hill. Once home to ranches and orchards, it's a good place to raise kids and ride horses.

This is where Gloria and Sebastian Santiago (not their real names) live and work. She's a trim, athletic fifty-eight-year-old with long, straight hair the color of sunflowers that bounces off her shoulders; he's a big guy with short gray hair, a gray mustache, and aviator-style glasses, still hearty at sixty-seven.

Their life together wasn't always idyllic. Back in 1998, at the age of forty, Gloria suddenly lost sight in one eye. "I was heading down to San Diego with our three sons and their friend, and I didn't want to disappoint them. So I got on the plane and we flew down to San Diego. By the time we landed I had no vision at all in the one eye," she recalls. Not knowing what to do, the fiercely independent woman rented a car and, with the four kids in tow, drove to the emergency room. "I drove one-eyed!" she says. "Of course I was terrified."

As she waited at the hospital, with four bored children clamoring to leave, Gloria imagined the worst—a brain tumor, perhaps a stroke. She called Sebastian, who was on a business trip to the Pacific Northwest. "I said, 'I think I have something serious!' And Sebastian's first response was, 'I suppose you'll be mad if I don't come down there.'"

Overhearing this story at the other end of our three-way phone call, Sebastian doesn't interrupt. But I do think I detect a quiet "mmm" from him. He doesn't deny a word of it.

Gloria continues, "Naturally, I reacted badly. I said something like, 'Never mind. I'll take care of it myself.'"

From that point on, in gradual steps, everything changed for them.

Gloria's eye slowly improved, but the next six months were grueling as she visited doctor after doctor in search of an explanation that would stick. Eventually she learned she had multiple sclerosis.

In essence, MS is a condition in which the body attacks its own central nervous system, causing inflammation and damaging the nerve fibers—thus interfering with the transmission of nerve signals. Because scientists haven't yet figured out the exact cause or target of the neurological attacks, MS is technically considered an "immune-mediated" disease—as opposed to an "autoimmune" disease. More than two million people worldwide have MS—perhaps many more, since it can go undetected for years—and there's no cure.

Who is likely to contract MS, and how is it contracted? Good questions that remain unanswered. Neither contagious nor inherited, it does appear to be most prevalent among women of European descent. Scientists are still trying to determine the precise causes.

So far, research has identified four types or courses of the disease. Most common—accounting for some 85 percent of new diagnoses—is the relapsing-remitting variety, characterized by a series of intermittent flare-ups, as the name implies. So far, it's the only type for which treatments such as interferon are available, and it's the type Gloria has. When in remission, some or all symptoms may vanish. That's the good news. The bad news: in most cases symptoms grow worse over time, morphing into what's called secondary progressive MS, in which neurological functioning steadily declines. Other types of MS include primary progressive MS, which involves a steady decline in functioning from the onset of symptoms, with no periods of remission; and clinically isolated syndrome, a twenty-four-hour bout of neurological distress that may or may not evolve into full-on MS.

MS itself isn't usually fatal. According to the National Multiple Sclerosis Society, people with MS tend to live on average about seven years less than the overall population, primarily because of preventable or manageable complications such as interactions between MS and other medical conditions—heart disease and stroke being chief among them.

Even when her MS went into remission and she felt fine again, the repercussions of Gloria's new reality—finding a smart and caring neurologist, figuring out her treatment options, living in fear of exacerbation and relapse—filled her life with unbearable stress. She abandoned her career as an executive headhunter for the high-tech industry in favor of something easier. She loves horses and she loves children, evidenced by her bachelor's degree in animal science from California Polytechnic State University and a teaching credential from a riding academy. So, in 1999, at forty-one, she became a horseback riding instructor at a nearby ranch.

There, at summer riding camp, Gloria was especially moved by a little girl with an inoperable brain tumor—specifically, how riding brightened the girl's attitude profoundly. This experience had a profound effect on Gloria too. She felt called to connect ill, disabled, abused, and other stressed kids with farm animals of all kinds.

Ten years later, in 2009, at age fifty, Gloria launched a horseback-riding therapy program. Today, it provides animal therapy to more than a thousand families annually—children with disabilities and/or life-threatening illnesses, veterans, homeless people, and other marginalized or at-risk folks. (Even more inspiring, Gloria works with rescued animals and offers her programs for free.) As executive director, she's "responsible for all facets of the nonprofit organization, including fundraising, animal care, program management, facilities management, accounting and marketing communications," explained the *Silicon Valley Business Journal* when it profiled her in April 2015.

"Reducing stress, being active rather than sitting in an office, and serving others have made a huge difference in my health," says Gloria. "On any given day," she told the *Journal*, "I may be cleaning horse stalls, driving goats to Ronald McDonald House, writing a grant and balancing the checkbook!"

I can see we have little in common. Shoveling horse poop? The healthy outdoor life? Not me. But in many other ways I was wrong, as I learn later.

Looking back, Gloria and Sebastian want me to know, her MS diagnosis almost seems like good news. "Before the doctors finally diagnosed what was wrong, it was a taxing and tumultuous time for us," she says. "We had some conflicts." (Read: fights.)

I'm confused about how the diagnosis eased those conflicts. I imagine that being told you have MS must be pretty traumatic, though I suppose if you've been expecting a brain tumor, perhaps it's not so bad. I recall that when my father-in-law first started seeing spots and other distortions, he felt relieved by one doctor's assertion that he'd probably had a mini stroke, meaning the worst was behind him. Unfortunately, what he actually had was cancer, and a couple months later he was gone. I drafted an essay called

"When a Stroke Is Good News," but I never had the heart to submit it for publication. The point: everything is relative, even diagnoses.

"It was scary in itself, the diagnosis, but not knowing was worse," explains Sebastian, who describes himself to me, in an earlier e-mail, as "True-blue American, former Marine. Semper Fi." A onetime deputy sheriff, he has the resonant voice of a radio announcer or airplane pilot. It's easy to imagine him as the 911 police dispatcher he's been for the past seventeen years, after leaving active duty. "It was definitely a relief to know exactly what was going on," he adds, "to be able to move forward and say, 'So now what do we do?'"

One of the first things they had to do—besides manage Gloria's career change—was find a good neurologist. This is a part of their story I can relate to personally. I know how hard it can be to find a specialist you click with, who gets you and whose recommendations you can follow. So I ask how their doctor search went. I hear Gloria groan.

"The first two neurologists I saw weren't helpful or kindly at all," she relates. "That's when I realized you really have to take your health care into your own hands. Not comfortable with a doctor—you need to find another one. It's kind of ironic that when you're at your weakest and most vulnerable is when you have to be your strongest advocate."

Tell me about it. We screen nannies and housekeepers and contractors, but somehow it's harder to flout the authority of the white coat. It's crucial to keep searching, though, to find someone you like, someone who basically tells the same story about your condition that you tell yourself. This is especially true, I think, if you're a cripple; medical professionals tend to pigeonhole us. Just because I'm quadriplegic, say, doesn't mean I need a suprapubic catheter, as I had to insist recently to a urological surgeon who wanted to operate. I then found another urologist who agreed with me and came up with a more agreeable solution to my middle-age prostate-related woes. (Thank you, Internet!) The web can help, but self-advocacy is the key.

In time, Gloria found a neurologist who, she says, "made a huge difference in my life." When she's having an MS flare-up— she's had three relapses since the initial episode, all starting with vision loss—Gloria immediately phones the neurologist. He puts her on an IV steroid—usually Solu-Medrol—which helps with the symptoms, if not the cause, of the disease. He also recommended weekly injections of Avonex, a type of interferon that can slow the disabling effects of certain types of MS—reducing the pace and extent of progression, decreasing the frequency of relapses, and actually lessening the number and size of brain lesions associated with MS. It was approved by the FDA in 1996, just two years before Gloria's diagnosis.

With it, her MS has been mostly in remission. "The doctor told us that only 5 percent of the population responds so positively to this injection, and Gloria is in that 5 percent," says Sebastian. "For whatever reason, whether it's her DNA or the age at which she was diagnosed or her lifestyle or whatever. We're extremely fortunate and grateful. It's really been a godsend."

Not that a weekly injection for the rest of your life is exactly fun. Originally it had to be mixed and shaken and poured into a syringe—"a giant pain in the *patoot*," says Sebastian. Now it comes in a premixed syringe. He knows, because he's responsible for giving it to her every week.

"In the beginning Gloria was doing it herself, but it got to the point where she just couldn't stand to stick a needle in herself anymore. So I've been doing it. In fact, sometimes I have to remind her, 'Hey, it's injection time.' She might say, 'I don't want to do this anymore!' Which I understand. It's a love-hate relationship, with the shot. But it's really helped keep her mostly symptom free."

"Sebastian now keeps a timer on his cell phone to remind us when it's shot night," Gloria puts in. "Otherwise I'd conveniently forget."

In fact, thanks to the injections and her switch to a healthy, low-stress lifestyle, most people who meet her don't even know she has MS. Not that it's a secret—and no, I'm not outing her. It's just that if you met her, you wouldn't notice.

Gloria isn't the only one who had a big post-diagnosis change; Sebastian did too. He strikes me as avuncular and kindly, but I gather that may not always have been the case. Sebastian enlisted in the Marine Corps straight out of high school, in 1968. He served a tour of duty in Vietnam and, upon his return, launched his law enforcement career. He was with the sheriff's office for nearly nineteen years, ten of which were in the K-9 unit (he loves dogs). All those years of physical exertion took a toll on Sebastian's body.

"My right shoulder was hyperextended on a number of occasions, causing permanent injury," he relates. "After two surgeries, the doctor told me I wasn't going to be able to continue as a deputy sheriff."

So he opened a coffee bar, but that didn't take. He missed his old uniform and responsibilities. After two years, he went back to the force and requested a reasonable accommodation. That's when he joined the local 911 department, where he works as a communications and records supervisor. (He also works part time at Gloria's therapeutic riding academy.)

That change—his own disability experience—wasn't easy either. "I'm dispatching now for officers who go out to the calls I used to go out to, which is an advantage because I can ask questions that I'd like to know myself if I were responding to a call," he tells me. "But then again, I'd also like to grab the keys and go out and take care of business—although I probably wouldn't last more than three hours because I'd get fired. . . . For me, this transition was difficult at first. But just like with Gloria's MS, it's gotten a lot better with time."

(I realize a two-disability couple goes against the rules of this book. But just because Sebastian is "disabled from active duty" doesn't mean his injury impacts his basic living activities in any measurable way. He also doesn't really rely on Gloria for any physical assistance, as she does on him.)

Nowadays, Sebastian rises at three a.m. and works twelve-hour days for half the week. He'd like to retire next year, to "spend more time with Gloria, going places and doing what we want," he says. At home, besides being on top of Gloria's weekly injections, he tends to most household chores. He takes care of the dog and two cats, does roughly half the laundry and most of the shopping, cooking, cleaning, and yard work. "I don't hire outside help," he says.

These family dynamics and the division of household labor have shifted a great deal since Gloria and Sebastian's wedding thirty years ago. "He's evolved," says Gloria. "He didn't have any previous experience with people with disabilities and wouldn't have described himself as nurturing or compassionate. But Sebastian's learned to be compassionate, supportive, and nurturing."

She goes so far as to say their shared experience with disability proved a boon to their marriage.

"After we worked through the challenges in the beginning, the MS diagnosis brought us closer as a couple," she says.

My jaw doesn't drop at that statement, but I do swallow hard. Her simple assertion echoes my own feelings about my disability's effect on my marriage. Though present from the beginning, my SMA has enabled M.L. and me to become closer—more tightly connected, communicating to each other the most intimate details of our daily lives—than many other disability-free couples we know.

Both Gloria and Sebastian were married to other people before becoming a couple, but they had known each other for years. They met when she was thirteen and he twenty-two, because Gloria's older sister married Sebastian's then roommate. Years later, that sister "played matchmaker when she learned we were both divorced single parents," Gloria explains.

At the time, of course, Gloria didn't have MS, and Sebastian's shoulder worked fine. But she did have a two-year-old son, and he had a three-year-old daughter.

"I knew Sebastian was the one when he said, 'We should get together and take the kids to the zoo sometime,'" she recalls. "Other people I dated always wanted me to 'find a sitter for the kid.'"

When next we talk, I ask Sebastian if he agrees that the MS diagnosis brought them closer as a couple. Gloria's assertion will only ring true to me if he concurs. Coping with big traumatic events can either tear you apart or bind you more tightly as a united front—being unchanged doesn't seem to be an option. Yet it strikes me that the person in danger—the one receiving help—is bound to feel closer to the other as a lifeline, if only in gratitude. If the person doing the extra work also feels enriched by the experience, then you've got something real.

"Well," he starts, "Gloria and I have been through a lot." He sighs. I note that big men sigh big. The gentleness that comes out of his mouth next feels big too, more sincere, more moving, because he *is* a big man. "But Gloria is the best thing that ever happened to me. I feel blessed every day to have her as my wife and partner."

There's a moment of dead silence.

"Anyway, we've been blessed with no exacerbations," he goes on, "and we're fortunate that our disabilities don't cut into our quality of life." He uses the plural—"disabilities"—because he's including his own joint problems. Besides the shoulder strain that got him reassigned at work, he's talking about his two hip replacements. "My shoulder is sore at times, but that's only when I do heavy activity," he says. Gloria has led the couple's efforts at healthy living through exercise and diet. "She's inspired me," he says. "I think we're aging well. We still enjoy going places and taking walks. I enjoy training and walking my German shepherd"—just sixteen months old, the puppy already weighs a hundred pounds—"and that helps keep me going."

Our next interview takes place a month later, after they get back from visiting a new grandchild and spending three weeks in Hawaii with another of their children, a son who's in the Air Force. They are indeed an active and busy couple, disabilities and all.

With their kids grown, Gloria and Sebastian are living in a kind of contented maturity, at least as long as her MS remains in remission. They acknowledge the helpful support of neighbors, friends, and family, especially in more difficult times. "In the beginning, people would come by and help around the house," says Gloria. The many flower bouquets were cheery, she adds, though perhaps most useful was when her sister drove her for a steroid injection during a relapse. (No more one-eyed driving excursions for her!) The kids, when they were younger, were perhaps more scared about Gloria's illness than they'd admit. "My son's best friend's father was also diagnosed with MS about a month before me, but he had a very aggressive form and passed away quickly," Gloria recalls. "So our kids were fearful at first." Gloria and Sebastian stressed to them how fortunate they were to have medicines that could help. "That's how we positioned it. That was our strategy. Now they don't even think about it," says Gloria.

Sounds like a good coping mechanism—accentuate the positive. I wonder if the Santiagos have other advice for couples going through similar situations. "Tips?" I ask. "Lessons learned?"

Sebastian takes the bait. "Be open to what's going on with your partner, and be as supportive as possible," he murmurs, his voice as smooth as molasses. "Because Gloria's right—I didn't get it at first. I mean, even at her worst, she looks fine! I didn't understand what was going on with her. You have to be open-minded enough to really listen, so you can assist with whatever needs to be done. Whether that's doing chores around the house or driving to the doctor—or just listening."

Gloria nods, her straight hair swinging slightly like a curtain in the breeze. "That's true," she says. "Also, always make your hopes and expectations clear. Verbalize them. Don't expect people to have ESP and know what you need, or there'll be disappointment and resentment." Yes, she goes on, during that first episode, when she called Sebastian from the ER in San Diego, he should've been more attentive and responsive. "But when he wasn't, I should've responded, 'Yes, please get on the next plane and be here. I need you.' But I was too proud and expected him to just know that's what I wanted. If I had to do it over, I'd say, 'Yes, I'll be mad if you don't come. Get your ass on the next plane!'" She laughs, but she means it. You can't hold people responsible if you don't tell them what you want and need, she reiterates. "Whether it's 'I'm feeling crappy today, could you please make dinner?' or just 'Could you come and hold me?' it's up to you to be able to verbalize whatever it is."

It strikes me that this is all good advice—for any relationship. Maybe folks who cope with disabilities really are ahead of the game. Maybe the disability experience gives them—*us*—insights into making relationships stronger.

But Gloria concedes that this wisdom only came gradually. "There was an evolution or metamorphosis. Neither of us was predisposed to be particularly compassionate or understanding of each other. But after thirty years of marriage, I feel like we're now closer and kinder to each other than ever." She then acknowledges that she wasn't "very compassionate or helpful" to Sebastian when he had to change careers due to his shoulder disability. "Retiring from active duty was life-changing for him," she says now.

Sebastian doesn't comment at first, not until Gloria asks him directly if what she's saying is accurate. Then he chuckles a moment before concurring. "Yeah, and I reacted badly and adjusted slowly," he says. "It's hard to be told something you've been doing for over twenty years . . . you can't do anymore." He adds that his hip replacements were almost as troublesome. "The hips weren't considered work-related—they happened after I was already retired because of my shoulder—but I'd say they were caused by the physical stresses of active duty," he says. "After two hip replacements and two shoulder surgeries, I actually forget about them sometimes, unless one starts acting up. But I am sort of the five-and-a-half-million-dollar man!"

Perhaps their individual disability experiences helped them react more sensitively to their partner's disability. But neither Gloria nor Sebastian will confirm or deny that supposition. In fact, I reflect, such sensitivity is not a given. Sometimes those who have suffered have no patience for others' suffering. I fear I myself have at times been unduly short with M.L. when she's tired or not feeling well—when her feet hurt from standing all day at work, and she simply wants to put them up and rest. It's hard when two people need attention or sympathy at once and neither one has the energy to accomplish anything. Worse still, if both of us catch cold at the same time, forget it!

So far such stressful moments have been short-lived, and we do make an effort to be understanding, to prioritize competing demands, and to be clear about our expectations and limits. What it'll be like when we're older, less patient, and have increasing needs, I can't say.

As our conversation winds down, Gloria declares, "Being diagnosed with MS has in many ways been a gift. It's made me appreciate the good things and not waste time or emotion on what doesn't matter."

"That's quite a statement."

"Well, honestly, I wouldn't change a thing about our lives, even if I could."

Better living through disability, as long as the disability is well managed and/or in remission. I can certainly attest to the fact that even at the worst times—or perhaps especially then—the disability experience can focus the mind. Sometimes I have to count every breath, every swallow of food—devote my full attention to surviving for the next fifteen minutes, say, until help arrives or the problem eases on its own. These perilous moments don't happen often, but they do happen. Each time, they make me angry and scared. Sometimes I stay angry and scared; these can be hard feelings to get rid of. Yet when they pass, they help me appreciate the ordinary. They prompt me to notice the small shifts in light and tone and feeling which I might otherwise ignore.

My inner cynic wonders if Gloria doth insist too much. A gift, MS—like something you'd give your friends? She clarifies that what she meant is that MS *brought* a gift: "It ultimately led me to found an organization to serve others, and it strengthened the relationship between Sebastian and me."

I hold my breath an extra second or two. You can't argue with success. Faced with mortality, or at least severe health-related limitations, Gloria and Sebastian restructured their lives, reprioritized. It strikes me as miraculous that the changes they made had such staying power and profound repercussions. Talk about making lemonade from lemons! Gloria's MS—and, to a lesser extent, Sebastian's shoulder injury—led them to reorient themselves in the world. I deplore the word "inspirational," because it's overused in regard to people with disabilities, but I can't help wondering if theirs is an example I could emulate.

Fat chance, I think. *We're so different*. Then again, I realize, perhaps I already have made lemonade. When I first became aware of how frustrating it can be to have a disability in a world built for the able-bodied—which was sometime after college, when I couldn't find a job and struggled to set up adequate personal assistance—I learned to channel my irritation into advocacy. All my effort was ostensibly to help the less fortunate, but honestly it fed a certain self-interest as well. I knew someday I might become less fortunate than I was then, and I had to turn what was beginning to feel like a liability—my disability itself—into an asset. Not to minimize or trivialize or negate the disability, as I had sought to do in my youth, but to *use* it. To leverage it. Disability gave me a cause, a voice, an identity—a disability pride that I could share.

"I feel the same way," Sebastian is saying.

As we wrap up our heart-to-heart, I imagine they must still have the occasional spat or stressful interaction. For them, I suppose, the rough times are just practice for improving their relationship. It's a good Zen kind of thought, but its brilliance will soon fade from my mind.

That very evening as I'm getting ready for bed—although M.L. and I have learned to try to express needs and wants with clarity and mutual respect—I grow cranky and impatient. "Can't you brush your teeth *after* you lift me into bed?" I snap.

She doesn't answer, maybe because she doesn't hear me. I have no fight in me, especially not over something so unimportant, so I don't bother to repeat my complaint (or was it a request?). We've supposedly learned better, yet how readily we revert to sullen, even resentful, brooding.

PART IV

TWENTY/TWENTY HINDSIGHT (THE LONG VIEW)

LAURIE AND J.R.

♦

THE HOLIDAYS ARE ALWAYS a hard time for those who depend on hired help. Personal-care assistants are entitled to join the hordes of the vacationing, of course, even if I don't. I rarely travel anymore, because of transportation access barriers, plus M.L. works in a gift boutique where Christmas shoppers are the life-blood of the business. So no breaks for us. But our household "staff"—if you can call one full-time worker and one part-timer a staff—deserves a respite. As I look around at the general disorder of my living room/office, I wonder, *Where does that leave me?* Frus-trated, and with a thousand small jobs that'll have to wait.

What I might ask is, *Where does this leave us?* Because this tem-porary gap in aid impacts M.L. too. She *is* my all-around, go-to backup. Even if it's the busiest time of year at her job.

This year's personal-care assistant—a nice young man from San Bernardino who graduated from UCLA and is applying to med school—is on two weeks' vacation. That's a long time, in my world. In fairness, he'd warned me about the trip even before I hired him. A prior obligation—he'd already bought the plane tickets. A capable, reliable, pleasant fellow, I'd felt fortunate to have him. So I'd said yes, okay, we'll manage somehow.

"Manage" meant one of two possibilities: find a temp replace-ment, which is next to impossible, or have M.L. pick up the slack in addition to her usual responsibilities. Here's how that lovely scenario works: she gets me washed and dressed and in my chair and fed in the morning, then sets me up at my computer. After she's showered and dressed, she gives me one last bathroom opportunity before going off to work. Fortunately, the shop where she works is just five minutes away and doesn't open till ten. About two hours later—at twelve-thirty, say—she returns home to give me a needed lunch-and-bathroom break. Then she repositions me at my computer, where I work (writing these very words) unassisted until she returns home again sometime after four p.m. During all this, our daughters—on school break—are either out with friends, working temp jobs of their own, or watching Netflix, though sometimes we get their help for small emergencies. I can also call M.L. at work, if need be—her boss is unbelievably understanding—but I won't unless it's absolutely necessary.

Under these circumstances, for much of my day there can be no unscheduled positional adjustments or spontaneous sips of water, no itch-scratching or sudden bathroom breaks. And for M.L., it's rush, rush, rush—which somehow is still never enough. I don't know which of us hates this short-term arrangement more, but I know who complains about it more: yours truly. No one should ever have his or her spouse as full-time attendant, if there's any choice about it.

Or so I believed until I met Laurie and Jacob "J.R." Hoirup of Sacramento.

Laurie, in her late fifties when we first encounter each other, sits comfortably cushioned in a well-used, somewhat battered motorized wheelchair. A hearty, forthcoming woman with a bushel of graying hair and obvious scoliosis, she's used a wheelchair since age five—an electric one since losing additional strength at thirteen. She holds a master's degree in rehabilitative counseling and a California teaching credential, and she worked for the state vocational rehab department assisting other disabled people until her recent retirement.

Her husband, J.R., a tall man with once-dark hair, hovers behind her at first, providing silent assistance. They've been married
eighteen years and started their relationship five years before that.

"I've been married twice," she says, her voice melodious and
friendly. "I'm a mother and now a grandmother, and J.R. is my
principal caregiver."

"Is that recent? Or you mean always?"

"Pretty much always," she says.

He nods in silent agreement.

Though statistics are imprecise, an increasing number of people do rely on family members—usually a spouse—for daily personal assistance. I wonder, can you keep love alive in a pressure
cooker like that? M.L. and I want *love* to be the secret sauce that
seasons our relationship, not need or duty. Not total dependency.

Laurie insists you can keep love alive. She insists she does.
That's part of her spiel. She frequently addresses audiences who
come to hear her motivational speeches and buy her autobiogra-
phy, *I Can Dance: My Life with a Disability*.

J.R. is more of an enigma. The job he has held longest has
been as Laurie's husband and helper. He's uncomfortable being
interviewed but not at all antagonistic. "J.R. was destined to be a
lifetime caregiver," Laurie is saying now.

"Destined?" I put it to him.

J.R. remains quiet for a long moment. I'm not sure if he's simply shy in general or protective about his life choices and feelings.
"I don't even know how to respond to that," he says finally. "It's
just something I did that worked for me."

Laurie sends me an essay she wrote about him and the term
"caregiver." It's not my favorite word—it sounds patronizing to
my cynical ears—but she defends it as a term of endearment. J.R.,
she writes,

> began providing care to people as a medic upon completion of
> diving school in his early 20s. As a professional diver, he worked
> with the speedboat racing circuit as rescue diver. . . . [Later] he

chose to do this for me because it worked for our lives. . . . Some would call him a saint, while others would consider him crazy, but I know that he is just a warm, caring individual who loves me very much. . . . I don't believe he intentionally set out to fall in love with someone who was going to need a caregiver for their entire life, but it happened.

Her description of J.R. and their relationship doesn't sound at all like M.L. and me, yet it rings a bell. M.L. didn't start as my (or anyone else's) attendant, but she *is* intrinsically a caring person. As I've said before, she's made a career of service to others: to me, to our kids, to her boss at the boutique. When M.L. was teaching in elementary schools, before having our own kids, she was once offered a position as school director and refused it, because she had no desire to be in charge, at least not in charge of other adults.

"In your twenties you were a rescue diver?" I ask J.R.

"I liked the excitement and the water," he answers. In college he worked part time assisting people with disabilities. "It was a job I could do that provided a place to live as well as income," he says. He also liked the lack of formal structure and the ability to be a friend to the people he was assisting. But he never worked more than six months with any one person—that's how he'd set it up, in advance—because he didn't want to feel hemmed in. By telling people upfront about his time limitation, he didn't have to feel guilty when he was ready to leave. He could feel free and responsible at the same time.

"He is loving and supportive, always putting others ahead of himself," Laurie wants me to know. If I had to guess, I'd never have said that Laurie and I share a diagnosis of SMA. Something in the way she holds her head and arms looks different to me from myself and other people I've known who have SMA. Perhaps it's because of her late onset. She was diagnosed at eighteen months and, at age two, began wearing leg braces and using crutches. Her atrophy began later than mine and progressed more slowly. She says she grows weaker every five or ten years.

J.R. doesn't have a disability, though he's increasingly coping with a variety of mild medical conditions that come with aging and that he declines to specify.

"We met when he answered an ad I'd put up for a caregiver," Laurie tells me in a subsequent phone call. "He had experience and excellent references, which is rare. So I was really impressed."

Before she hired him, though, she had to introduce him to her two kids from her first marriage—a son, age eight, and a daughter, four. Her kids "took to J.R. wonderfully," she recalls. Within a few months, however, a problem arose. She and J.R. became attracted to each other. "My rule about male caregivers was never get involved romantically because that can ruin the caregiver situation," she says.

I laugh. For many of us it goes the other way around: we don't want our lovers to become our personal-care assistants, for fear that will ruin the romance.

At that point, she says, she had to let J.R. go because she was falling for him. She found different help. "J.R. and I remained close friends," she says. In fact, he became her boyfriend. But he was still at loose ends professionally, so in time he moved back in as both assistant and lover. A few years later they tied the knot.

Though he'd assisted disabled people before, he had no previous romantic experience with them. He'd also never been married and had no kids of his own.

"But you, Laurie, had been married before," I prompt.

Her first husband, John, was also able-bodied. "John was gay, I think, though of course I didn't know that at the time," she says. "It's possible he married me in order to have kids, and he figured that with someone with a disability, the sexual component wouldn't be a prominent issue. At least that's my analysis. We were both quite young."

Her analysis seems flawed to me, since a woman with an inherited disability doesn't seem like the most obvious candidate for reproduction. Maybe it was more a matter of experimentation;

they were both in their early twenties, after all. In any case, she got pregnant right away.

"The doctors weren't sure how long I'd be able to endure pregnancy. But I figured once I had a family everything would be great. The pregnancy went fine, and a few years later we had a second child. But by the time *she* was two, I was done with the marriage. I was thirty-two when I decided to get out of it."

I can tell she's struggling to explain a difficult, distant memory. She knows the problems with her first marriage probably weren't entirely his fault.

"Part of it was my own naïveté, my desire to be married and my denial about the warning signs," she reflects. "But by the time I'd passed thirty I realized there was no hope. This was not going to work. And it took a few more years to actually separate."

Laurie grew up in northern Illinois, in a small town where she attended regular schools. She always had friends, she says, and even dated in high school. "All able-bodied folks. And I never really thought about what was going to happen in the future." Her parents, however, did send her to a summer camp sponsored by the Muscular Dystrophy Association. "I remember people telling me, 'Wouldn't it be cute if you got together with somebody else in a wheelchair?' And I remember thinking, *No, it wouldn't! What could we do for each other?* It would really be quite a difficult situation. Not that I avoided other people with disabilities. I went out with guys in chairs, but it aggravated me when people said how cute we were."

She moved to California to attend California State University at Sacramento, where she says she dated more nondisabled guys. I don't ask her exactly what she means by "dated," whether that included sex. But I do wonder at her ability to attract men, including *two* husbands, when so many folks with disabilities struggle with loneliness.

"I never had trouble attracting guys," she says. "I'm not a wallflower. I never rolled into a bar and had strangers offer to buy me a drink or anything, but I was always friendly. Most of the guys I dated started as friends. It wasn't the look-across-the-room kind of thing. But I was probably fairly assertive. I never waited for them to come to me. Plus I was attracted to certain older men, so that helped keep things at a level of maturity."

John, her first husband, had been her upstairs neighbor in her first apartment after college.

"We met at the pool and started hanging out, going to movies, bowling. After several months we moved in together and soon got married."

"Fast work," I hear myself say.

"It was a mess!" she chuckles. "Well, it was good for about seven months. I was happy—I had a ring! But then it quickly started going downhill. He never abused me physically or anything like that, but there was emotional abuse, and I don't know how far it would've gone if I'd let it. I got out before I was in grave danger."

I make a concerned sound.

"He also threatened me through my kids," she continues. "If I didn't love him, I'd never get to see my kids."

Somehow she did manage to separate from John and keep her kids. She had enough help with parenting and "caregiving," as she would say, from friends and family to pull it off. John had been her sole personal-care assistant. "Was that part of the tension?" I ask. "His personal-care role?"

"He'd insisted on it," she says. "He wanted nobody else to help me. It was, I think, part of his control-freak thing. To keep me under his control."

I have a fantasy about getting to interview John for his side of the story. But alas, Laurie tells me, he vanished years ago. I think I can almost relate to the control-freak characterization. When M.L. and I were first together, I wanted to know all about her comings and goings. I worried incessantly and unnecessarily about other guys, for no reason and without provocation. I was possessive, insecure. Similarly, she didn't want me to hire any female attendants, out of some kind of jealousy—and I never have, though lately she says it'd be okay. Laurie's story, however, sounds dangerous. There are abusive attendants, just as there are abusive spouses.

"It was a really difficult time," she says. "I got sole custody of both kids and pretty much decided I was going to be alone. It'd take an unusually special person to accept having a partner with not only a disability but two small children! But I decided I'd rather live happily alone than unhappy in a miserable relationship."

She gave herself time to heal, she says. Two years, to be exact. When she interviewed J.R. to become her attendant, he said it would only be temporary (as was his custom).

"He was at the point of being burned out on the whole caregiving thing," Laurie recounts. When he started working for her, he planned to dabble in a side business of fixing used cars in her garage. Maybe. He was, in truth, a drifter (his word) with no particular goal or future in mind. "Once *I* started working full-time," she says, "J.R. really only had to be my caregiver in the morning and at night, because I was gone all day long, which gave him time to do his own things."

Laurie insists the custodial arrangement never cramped their love life. They still enjoy time together, especially camping or watching TV. They visit their grandkids frequently. They have four, two from each child.

"J.R. never had any children of his own, though he considers my kids his own," she says. "When he was younger, he thought about it, but by the time we got together I'd already had a hysterectomy. We discussed adopting, but he decided that helping raise my two would work just fine for him."

As a stepdad, he was involved in Boy Scouts and father-daughter dances at school, among other things. "I'm still close with them," says J.R., "and now I love being a grandpa even more."

What might cramp their style, though, is age. Laurie needs more physical help than she used to—she keeps growing weaker, thanks to her SMA—and he's become somewhat less able to provide it, thanks to his being nearly sixty. Both have less energy.

Plus she's retired from work, so she's home all day now and J.R. has less freedom. Still, they manage to negotiate through competing needs.

"How?" I ask. "Any tips?"

"I drink to cope with the stress," says J.R.

"He uses a lot of humor," Laurie comes back.

She says it's a matter of being respectful of each other's needs and wants. If he wants to go bike riding, say, she knows she has to make some other arrangement to ensure her needs are met, perhaps even hiring short-term part-time help (though usually she can find the help she needs from friends, neighbors, and her now grown-up kids). At home, she can work independently at her computer, which frees him up.

"But there *are* difficulties," she acknowledges. "He knows he's always on call, and that can be stressful. Even if he's doing his own thing, he knows if I need something, he's got to come and help me. . . . He's human and gets overwhelmed at times, but he always manages to push through."

"And if he complains, you don't get offended, Laurie?"

"We both try to be considerate of one another and support each other," she says. "I used to think it took a special kind of person to be married to someone like me, but I don't think that anymore. Instead, I think you fall in love with the person you fall in love with, and you deal with whatever that entails."

I find myself wishing there were another way. The scenario Laurie is painting is all too familiar. I hate knowing M.L. can never fully relax because she's always on call. She's well aware you can never count on hired help, at least not completely. There's good help and bad help, but there's nothing or no one as reliable and loyal as she. That's a trust I dare not take advantage of. I hope she, knowing this—knowing I do my best to be as autonomous as possible, not to abuse her helpfulness, her love—will feel a kind of love and even protection in return, from my trust in her.

I ask J.R. how he feels about being in that role. He answers slowly. "It helps that we were good friends first."

I ask for an example of how they work out the compromises.

"He likes to go to bed early, and I don't," says Laurie. "Sometimes I will anyway, and sometimes I'll stay up on my computer while he's asleep. But then I have to wake him up later to put me in bed. We experiment to see what works best, which can vary on any given night."

On their wedding night, she tells me, one of her best friends helped get her into her nightie and set an amorous scene while the friend's husband took J.R. out for a beer. That way J.R. didn't have to do double duty as attendant and groom. More recently, they took hired help on a three-month driving trip to hawk her memoir. "It was a lot of extra work, loading and unloading boxes of books as well as getting me ready for presentations, so we took along an older woman who could kind of entertain herself," says Laurie. "But at other times we've taken vacations where we didn't want somebody else coming along for the ride. It really depends."

Later, I ask her privately if this balancing act ever reached a particular low point—and if so, how did they resolve it? She says J.R. hasn't had a weekend to himself in more than twenty years, and "there was a point when he felt he'd like to just have a regular job and let somebody else do my care," she tells me.

"What happened?" I assume they had to hire more helpers. But that's not exactly what she says.

"We actually split up for a month or two because of it."

"You mean he wanted a complete change of lifestyle? Not just a break on the caregiving?"

She responds so quickly I'm not even sure she heard me. "But we continued to talk," she says. "Over time he decided he really wasn't happy on his own."

This answer strikes me as facile. Problems like that don't get resolved so quickly. She seems to be saying J.R.'s caregiving responsibilities and their romantic life together are so intertwined as to be almost indistinguishable. I put it to her, only not in so many words.

"Yes, but not really," she responds. "I know he's under strain from the caregiving, but that's separate from our love life." I struggle to grasp this distinction, to formulate my next question. In the meantime, she elaborates: "One time I wanted to give him some days off, as a surprise. So I stayed with my now-adult daughter for four days. She can take care of me. But after just two days J.R. called and begged me to return home. 'I don't want to be alone,' he said. I had to urge him to use the time for himself."

I can't help wondering if that's just her version—if it suits her to believe she's more independent than he is, in a way. So later, I check the story with him. It's true, he says, except for one key detail. "There was no *begging*," he says with a teasing chuckle, his voice resonant, oxygenated. "I told her it was okay and I didn't need her to be away; she could come back anytime she wanted. But no, there wasn't any begging on my part. That's just Laurie's interpretation. She likes to tell it that way."

I laugh with him. I think I'm beginning to see the mutuality or symbiosis of their relationship. Just as he gives her the mobility and personal assistance she needs, so too does she provide him with something essential to his well-being—an agenda, a context, perhaps, even a schedule or structure, and, I suppose—judging by his characteristic taciturnity—a voice. (I may often provide M.L. with structure and purpose, but *never* a voice!) Theirs seems a truly reciprocal relationship.

Days go by during which I contemplate our conversations. It occurs to me that Laurie and J.R.'s relationship, interdependent as it is, also carries a depth of cooperation and shared understanding. To the outsider their relationship might appear to bend under a never-ending strain, but to them, when it works, there's a kind of rhythmic hum, a harmony . . . a blending of two lives. The next time we talk I ask, point-blank, "Do you find spending so much time with your husband to be a strain, or do you develop a special understanding, an uncommon degree of closeness?"

She thinks it over, but not for long. "Most couples, one or both partners go off to work, and they only come together in the evenings or weekends. They have little time to be together, and even then, they're busy doing laundry or other housework or taking care of the kids. You've heard the jokes about people who, when they retire, realize they don't actually know or like the person they've been married to all these years. *That will never be us.* I guess to spend so much time together, you really have to like the person, not just love him or her."

I make affirmative, encouraging noises. "So disability doesn't take away from a good marriage?" I say. Just checking.

"It may be different if one partner suddenly gets a disability, putting a new strain on the relationship. But if one of the parties already has a disability before entering into the relationship, and the able-bodied partner knows that in advance, then they already know what to expect. They know what's there, so it's not a shock."

Fair enough. But her disability has worsened with age, and J.R. has become less able to do certain tasks for her. "Still, there are always unexpected developments, no?" I say.

"Sure," she answers. "You know, I'd like to write a book about aging with a disability. Of all the stuff that's available for seniors in general, none of it really addresses someone with a significant preexisting disability."

Tell me about it. Even doctors are little help in informing us about old age for folks like Laurie and me, who once would have died before reaching fifty. So nobody really knows what to expect. It never ceases to sadden me when I think about how I can't caress M.L. the way I used to, since my skin-and-bone hands have become too weak. In time I'm destined to don a ventilator mask à la some sci-fi villain, I'm told. But let's face it, M.L. isn't the energetic gung-ho girl she used to be either. That's the bargain we make: age together—gray hair, wrinkles, atrophy, and all. (Heck, our wedding song was "Grow Old with Me.")

Laurie acknowledges they'll soon have to reduce J.R.'s load. "At the moment we only have an aide on weekday mornings. J.R.

is doing the rest. But at some point we'll need to use a Hoyer lift, rather than having him just pick me up, and hire and train someone else to fill in more hours."

How they will afford that is another question. "We used up my retirement fund," she says. "We've turned part of our house and garage into a little apartment, to offer room and board for several hours' work. But that's only worth so much. I'm not sure what we're going to do as we need more and more hours. I'm looking into whether I can qualify for Medi-Cal [California's Medicaid program] and the Working Disabled Program, which would allow me to do small part-time jobs without losing benefits."

She trails off. I'm numb thinking about the financial reality. Numb and angry. The Working Disabled Program is one of those workarounds enacted years ago after advocates protested work disincentives in the benefits programs. WDP essentially allows qualified disabled people who can pay a low monthly premium to be eligible for Medi-Cal if their total net income amounts to less than 250 percent of the federal poverty level. They can also waive some of the income limits for SSI. This is considered progress, though there's still an inherent work disincentive. Where are we as a society if people who *can* work are afraid to work too much because, by working, they risk losing necessary life-sustaining benefits?

"If I could change one thing about my situation, it would be to have more help," she goes on. "I'd like to take more of the burden off J.R. I wish there were more good people available to do whatever, so we wouldn't have to do so much planning just to give him time off. Yes, more money for more hired help would be terrific!"

It's never easy to find good assistants. Online ads cast too wide a net. Postings at local colleges, medical centers, and coffee shops can be too narrow. Agencies charge too much and don't necessarily deliver better candidates. When I'm hiring, I try to convey authority and organization—not neediness. It's a job, not charity. I've asked M.L. to join me in interviewing applicants—we're in this together, I'll say—but she prefers not to. She's explained she doesn't want the attendant to think, as some of them do, that he's working for *her*, that *she's* hiring him to take care of me. She wants to make it clear from day one that I'm in charge, directing my own care. She's right. That's important. Nevertheless, I always make a point of introducing her, just to test out how the applicant reacts to her and vice versa. (She can always veto my selection, after all.) If I hire him, they're bound to interact sooner or later, and I prefer to make sure their first meeting is in my presence.

I ask Laurie about her hiring process. "We hire together," she says, "because I want candidates to know I'm not home alone. They need to know they can't take advantage of the situation— and if they mess up, they're going to be fired because I've got backup right here. But the final hiring and firing decision is always up to me."

Makes sense, but for me it's different. I don't want my attendants to assume M.L. will cover for them if they get lazy, as many of them do. I prefer that my attendants realize that they'll leave me in the lurch if they disappear. Guilt goes a long way toward inspiring responsibility. Also, I'd prefer they assume I have to hire someone else when they don't do the job—someone who will cost me money they could've had.

"It's kind of funny," Laurie is saying, "but one thing J.R. always tells my caregivers is, 'You need to realize *she's* your boss, not me. She's articulate and knows what she wants.'" I couldn't agree more, though I favor delivering that message myself. The worst thing, we concur, is people with professional training or any kind of nursing license. "They come in with a mindset like, 'This is how I was trained. I know what's best,'" says Laurie, echoing my experiences.

Trouble finding and keeping simpatico aides is perhaps the number one complaint among people like us, I've found. Ideally, a good personal-care assistant can become like a best friend and trusted confidant. At worst, an abuser. You lay yourself open and are incredibly vulnerable bringing strangers into your home, your bedroom and bathroom. But I've had helpers from all over the world and all socioeconomic levels, and I've enjoyed getting to know about unfamiliar cultures—though there are undoubtedly advantages to having an assistant with whom you share cultural reference points. It would be nice if our society would produce more qualified people for this kind of work and provide the means to pay them adequately. It would be nice if this kind of work weren't looked down upon as "unskilled domestic labor" but, rather, seen as a noble service or even a fulfilling career. (I hear good personal-care assistants are easier to find in England, where they're called "carers," but I don't know firsthand.) But sadly, as I've often joked with M.L., what can we expect from wipers of other people's bottoms? We have to have realistic (read: low) expectations, even while hoping for the best.

I end my conversation with Laurie feeling deeply grateful for my parents' insistence that I, from an early age, learn to direct my attendants myself—and for their ability to provide me the financial resources to do that. In those rare times when I'm between paid assistants (or it's a holiday vacation, and temporary), when M.L. does fill in as my assistant, it's entirely by our choice, not necessity. That's a freedom I can never forget or take for granted.

(Author's note: Not long after this was written, Laurie Hoirup died in a tragic accident. I'm grateful to her family for allowing me to publish her thoughts and observations about her life with J.R.)

CHRISTINA AND JANET

———◆———

ONE SPRING AFTERNOON, resisting an almost overwhelming yen to nap at my computer, I happen upon an online review of a new memoir by a disabled woman. Touted to be unsentimental and frank about loss and pain and, more importantly to me, about how her longtime romantic relationship reshaped itself around her disability, the book was in my Amazon cart without a second thought.

Further piquing my interest as I dug into the hardcover volume a few days later—I prefer hardcovers, as a rule, for their inherent bookishness, though e-books are obviously easier since they don't require someone else (usually M.L.) to turn pages for me—was the fact she'd had a spinal cord injury at age fifty! I'd thought SCIs were the province of younger folks—daredevils who drove too fast or drank too much or climbed too high or had reckless friends who caused their injuries. When a more mature person becomes disabled, I generally assume it's from Parkinson's, MS, Alzheimer's, or even cancer.

How wrong I was.

Six weeks later, when I first dial Christina Crosby's cell phone, after a brief e-mail exchange, she answers warmly, then apologizes and asks if we can postpone. "The refrigerator repairman is here," she says, "and we *really* want our fridge fixed." It's noisy and distracting, the repair work, and might impinge on the privacy necessary for frank discussion. Of course I don't mind, I say, finding this a touching example of the domesticity she shares with her partner, Janet Jakobsen. We reconnect later that afternoon.

Here's what I know going in: Christina, sixty-two at the time we speak, is a professor of English and feminist, gender, and sexuality studies at Wesleyan University, in Middletown, Connecticut, and author of the memoir *A Body, Undone: Living On After Great Pain*. In October 2003, she suffered a severe bicycling accident—a twig got caught in one of her spokes, sending her flying. Yes, a twig. "My chin took the full force of the blow, which smashed my face and broke the fifth and sixth cervical vertebrae in my neck," she writes. "The broken bone scraped my spinal cord." The hyperextension of her neck caused an "incomplete" (meaning her spinal cord was scraped, not severed) injury at the C5–C6 level. Today, she has severe paralysis in her trunk and legs, with just enough function in her arms and hands to drive an adapted minivan. She uses a standard wheelchair, speaks clearly, although her breathing is sometimes strained, and has zero bladder or bowel control. She also copes with ongoing physical pain throughout her body.

At the time of the accident, she and Janet had already been living together for six years. Janet, seven years Christina's junior, is a professor of women's, gender, and sexuality studies at Columbia University's Barnard College, in New York City. So when we first speak, they've been an item for more than nineteen years. Neither is interested in getting legally married, however, given the connubial history of paternalism, as Christina explains in her book—the "contracting" of a wife as a man's personal property. Furthermore, they say, they're not keen on turning a private, voluntary commitment into a government-validated obligation.

I understand, but it makes me smile. After so many have fought so hard and so long for marriage equality, which this couple supports, the institution itself still isn't to everyone's taste. The right to marriage isn't an obligation to marry, after all. Still, it's only fair to have the option. Equal access, freedom of choice—the principles go hand-in-hand.

Christina's writing, like her manner of speech, is suffused with this style of analytical thinking and professorial lingo. One particular passage from her book becomes the basis of my first question. It describes an argument she and Janet had shortly after Christina returned from the hospital all those years ago:

> I wanted the window shade in the front window of the living room to be straightened, because it bugged me when the shades weren't evenly positioned. I wanted to know if the mechanism was in some way damaged. I wanted it to be fixed. The misalignment didn't bother Janet, she may not even have noticed it, but now I was asking her to add the shade to the endless and ever growing to-do list that she carried around in her head. I was demanding her labor, and I was driving her crazy, as she was making patently clear. Yet all the fight went out of her when I said, "I want it," without any further justification. . . . Janet told me, very truly and not in wrath, but with a terrible finality, "You can't have what you want. You just can't." There's no way that she can respond to every wish of mine for this or for that—even if she has the skill, she may not have the inclination, and she certainly doesn't have the time.

I positively tingle reading this passage. I too like things aligned and symmetrical and balanced, and I get impatient about fixing them. But I know—have always known—that I can't have everything I want. My mother made that clear when I was young. "You want what you want when you want it, but that's not how the world works," she'd say. It still resonates in my brain.

On the phone, I ask Christina, "You write that you were in your early fifties when you learned you can't always have everything you want, but don't most people learn that when they're, oh, about two?"

She laughs. Good—I haven't pissed her off. Maybe I've gauged her personality more or less accurately from the photographs I've seen of her seated in a dark-colored wheelchair, a pleasant-looking woman with unfussy bobbed gray hair and glasses, and the big-boned physique of a former amateur athlete. "Yes," she says. "But so many household jobs I used to do suddenly became Jan's. For example"—she inhales pensively—"Janet now manages all of our bills, the business end of our life. I call her the CEO and CFO of our household operation."

Christina's voice is soft. Her words, delivered slowly, surprise me. For me and some other crips I know, paying bills is one of the tasks we contribute. It's relatively sedentary and, for me at least, accessible via computer—it's a job M.L. hates anyway and probably wouldn't tend to do well on her own. (She says so herself.)

"Before I was hurt," Christina goes on, "we shared our resources but didn't merge our accounts. Each of us managed her own money. Each kept track of her own bills." Besides working at different universities, she explains, they have two homes—an apartment in New York, near Barnard, and a house in Middletown, near Wesleyan. "We jointly own both places, but it was easy to imagine two different households. That's gone now," she says. "Janet really does everything."

"Yes," Janet agrees. I envision her—tall, in pictures, perhaps perched near Christina's chair, with an ever-ready grin, graying hair hanging loosely to just below her broad shoulders. Perhaps she's tucking a few wisps behind an ear.

"By 'everything,' you don't just mean laundry and other housework?" I query.

"Right. The big stuff," Christina says. "It's hard for me physically to handle all the materials [and] equally difficult to keep track of details. The medications I take really erode my mental capacity."

I know she's on prescription drugs for chronic pain, which can torpedo one's ability to concentrate or think clearly. I wonder which is worse for her—loss of physical ability or loss of mental capacity. "But you don't really miss those chores, do you?" I say. When there's no response, I add, "Or did you enjoy paying bills?"

"I enjoyed being *able* to," she comes back. "It's a matter of control, isn't it? Being able to do what you want. Jan and I each had our own operation, so to speak. I was my own person. That's a lot to give up."

I can't help thinking everyone has to give up something. A dream, an activity, a loved one. Sooner or later, we all must face limitations and disappointments. We all suffer losses. To be disabled is to wait, to lack control, to know powerlessness—but frustrating as that may be, it's not altogether bad. It forces you to let go and gets you off the hook from a lot of obligations. It frees you of many duties and responsibilities. And if you're lucky, in time, you may enter what theologian Reinhold Niebuhr famously termed "the serenity to accept the things I cannot change." In other words, a state of grace. But I say none of this.

"What about you, Janet?" I say instead. "How has Christina's disability changed your life, if at all?"

She hesitates. "I can't always have everything I want either," she says at last. "There are things Christina and I used to be able to do together, all kinds of activities I can't do anymore because they require two people or because my enjoyment of them came from doing them together."

She talks more quickly than Christina but no less thoughtfully. I ask for an example of these shared activities.

She and Christina were—and to an extent still are—outdoorsy types: hiking, kayaking, bicycling, cross-country skiing. I'm reminded that bicycling is what caused Christina's accident. It's one of the cruel ironies that so many SCI quads *were* athletic, which is how they got injured in the first place. I myself have always been resolutely *in*doorsy. "One reason I married you is I knew you'd never take me camping," M.L. quips from time to time.

"Until we reorganized our leisure time," Christina is saying, "it was always around physical activity. For us that was a very big loss."

Could I be forgiven for thinking there are bigger losses in life? Surely there are accessible hiking trails, rugged all-terrain wheelchairs, and leisure sports such as skiing and surfing that have been adapted for paraplegics and quadriplegics.

"So what do you do instead, in your leisure time?" I prompt.

"We've taken up museum going," Janet offers, "which is kind of like hiking only indoors with hard, flat floors and art on the walls to look at instead of trees. And we spend more time in the garden at our house in Middletown. Christina can come out on the deck, when the weather allows."

Museums are great, I almost say. For me, they've never been entirely about the cultural aspects so much as the wide, smooth rolling spaces. As a kid in New York, I loved getting lost at the Met, once I got my motorized wheelchair. Or at least I'd *feel* lost, zooming down corridor after corridor until I no longer knew which way I'd come. The freedom I felt moving through the capacious exhibits was magical.

"We've tried," Janet continues, "to find other activities to replace the ones we used to enjoy but—and this is odd, because we really have a very pleasurable life—even all these years later I still deeply miss those activities. I'm not even in Christina's position of having had to relinquish so much, but it's hard. I'd thought we'd just develop new activities and it'd be fine, but the loss is still painful. I guess people really aren't so fungible."

For a moment it's difficult to hear her. Her voice trails off. Christina punctuates the silence. "The loss can be excruciating!" she puts in.

How do they handle the frustrations? What keeps them from bickering with each other over these and other shared aggravations? Their answers are complex and surprising. "One of the traits that helps is generosity," says Janet. "And of the two of us, Christina is the more generous, since she *has* to be patient pretty much all the time."

I work this idea through my brain. Does it count as generosity if she really has no choice?

Janet goes on: "She has to decide whether to tell me about her needs. She has to be patient if I'm not able to help right away or if I don't understand. That takes generosity, and there are all kinds of things she has to be generous about as we go through the day and I try to assist her."

I'm liking what Janet is saying—that the one receiving help has to be at least as generous as the one giving it. Or should be. I know sometimes I'm not very generous with M.L. I become grumpy if she can't do what I want her to do right away—as when she stops to file a fingernail and I want her to give me a sip of water first. By the same token, she may snap at me when she feels overwhelmed. But usually we understand what's going on and forgive each other. That too is an expression of generosity. Mutual generosity could be the crux of successful interabled relationships—or any relationship, for that matter.

To understand better how they balance Christina's requests and Janet's constraints of time and patience, I bring up the example of the crooked window shades from Christina's book. Christina says the way they've negotiated through such "rough spots" is by implementing what she dubs the feminist notion of *process*. "It's important to go over what happened," she explains, "to ask, *What just happened?* And try to figure it out and not just brush it away or get over it or try not to have it happen again. To look at it and understand the process. That way, every fight becomes a learning experience, and conflicts can actually bring us closer."

They learned to do this—separately, pre-relationship, and together—by working with feminist organizations that were "run by consensus," Christina says. For instance, as a graduate student she worked with a group that ran a shelter for battered women. "A collective," she corrects herself, "that had our meetings by consensus."

Consensus building and stress analysis sound like good and sound processes to employ in any relationship. My mind rushes back to when I was a kid at school—how, when there was no one to ask for help if I had to pee or was suffering from some other minor but intimate discomfort—no one I was comfortable being vulnerable in front of, I'd learned to do without, to endure. At times I'm glad of that early training. For me, even as an adult, suffering in silence is sometimes necessary. I can't always count on prompt assistance whenever my nose itches or a butt cheek falls asleep. But stoicism is no way to build a relationship. So when M.L. entered my life, I had to unlearn that macho self-discipline, temper that stubborn self-denial. I had to stop being uncommunicative about my sundry discomforts.

At first, M.L. was genuinely invested in trying to resolve all my requests, but we both soon discovered that it's just not possible. We discovered we had to distinguish between authentic urgent needs and postponable or ignorable wishes and whims. I had to be clearer about my immediate situation, and she had to learn to say, "I'm not able. I'm too tired. Can it wait? Can you call someone else?"

It's not a formal process, but it is a means to greater and shared self-awareness. Or at least it is when it works, when we remember to be fair and generous and patient. And when we have the mental and physical wherewithal.

Into my speakerphone, I read aloud a passage from Christina's book: "It's a testament to the sheer durability of our feelings for each other that the love that was so vital and alive before the accident survived without a scratch." Then I say, "A lot of couples feel deep love but can't stay together after a traumatic event like yours. So does love alone explain your longevity as a couple?"

"Well, there are other qualities that shore us up. Financial resources, for one," answers Christina. "We have money to pay for help, which many others don't."

Christina is able to manage on her own through most of the day, but her aide, Donna, comes every morning for about four hours to help her get showered and dressed. Donna also administers her twice-weekly bowel program—manually flushing out shit—and changes her suprapubic catheter every two weeks, which is the external cath for voiding the bladder. Donna helps with occasional "stander" therapy too, getting Christina into and out of a device that locks her into a vertical position for a time, to improve her circulation and bone density, among other purported benefits. "But once I get to my computer, Donna can leave [and] I go to work," says Christina. Some days Christina has to leave the house to teach a class or attend a faculty meeting. "When I come home, there's nobody there. I get my own food and put myself to bed."

Donna has been helping Christina since she got out of the hospital twelve years ago. I've never had a personal-care assistant last anywhere near that long. They clearly have a good relationship. But when Christina is in New York, or when Christina and Janet travel, Janet does all the personal care. So I ask if they ever wish they had more hired help—or less, for that matter, for more privacy. "Always the trade-off," Christina muses, without really answering.

"We're truly fortunate," says Janet then. "The balance between getting help and maintaining privacy is probably the best it can be, given Christina's needs."

Even when they don't use Donna, they pay her so she has "the security of a steady income," Christina tells me in a subsequent interview. Which, no doubt, also helps breed loyalty. (I'm taking notes, wondering if I'm fair to my own paid assistants!)

Christina and Janet understand how fortunate they are, in part, because of Christina's late brother, Jeff, who had a progressive form of MS. They witnessed his decades-long struggle with declining muscle control all the way through to his death, which was shortly after Christina's injury. "I saw Jeff being cared for by aides who came from an agency," Christina recalls. "Some of them were affectionate and enjoyed being in Jeff's presence but not all of them. And there was a transience to it. People frequently just took off." She adds that she and Janet are "fortunate to be able to pay directly for help without going through an agency."

I know exactly what she means; I'm privileged in the same way. The problem is, agencies that provide "certified home health aides" charge a lot, first of all, yet pay the actual laborers about half of that. If you can hire on your own, you can spend less and usually secure a higher quality worker. But Medicaid and private insurance carriers often only work with agencies. (The specific limits and regulations vary by state, but there is a movement to push Medicaid toward more consumer-directed hiring choices.) Home health agencies are accredited and know how to bill insurers, though I've found that independent first-time assistants are flexible and want to learn. More importantly, an assistant whom you hire and pay personally is beholden to you. You're the boss, not the assigned "patient du jour." It's a different feeling, a different kind of relationship.

One of the saddest aspects of Jeff's story, as laid out in Christina's book, is that in his final years his marriage fell apart. His disability may have played a role in that dissolution, so I ask Christina and Janet about it and what they may have learned about relationships from this example.

Christina answers first. "I think Jeff had a hard time understanding he may have been asking too much of his family. He simply assumed they'd help him, the family unit would provide the labor he needed, and it took them too long to realize they had to set up a separate support system." She pauses. "Yes, after I got hurt, we had ample warning that we'd better figure out the new home economics quickly."

Then Janet shares two stories. For fifteen years she was head of the Barnard Center for Research on Women, where she led symposia on disabilities in a social/political context. "Disability is taken up a lot in feminist thought," she informs me. "So I was certainly aware of some of the issues people face."

But that, she freely admits, was mostly theoretical. Political, not personal.

More intimate knowledge came from the experience of a college roommate whose father had MS and whose mother, a professional nurse, assisted him at home till the end—which, after Christina's injury, Janet recalled as an "inspirational" example.

"Theirs was a home full of love," she says now.

Christina and Janet own up to having other advantages as well. "The material structure of our lives is extremely helpful," says Janet. "We both have flexible jobs, so I can shift my teaching schedule to afternoons and do care for her in the mornings. That kind of thing."

They also credit ongoing support from family and friends. Yet surely not everybody has been supportive, I say, having heard about and experienced enough awful behavior to know what I'm talking about. But Christina insists no one who knows them has expressed surprise over their staying together post-injury. "What about strangers?" I query, undeterred.

"It's true, our union isn't always immediately legible," Christina allows. "One of the things I hate most is when we're not taken as a *sexual* couple." This was often the case even before her injury. Perhaps they don't fulfill enough lesbian stereotypes for some observers to see them as sexual partners. (In her book, Christina jokingly refers to herself as "butch-femme" and Janet as "femme-butch," a distinction without much difference and utterly lost on the general public.) What's different now is some strangers make too much fuss. "The inspirational stuff is just ghastly," is how Christina puts it.

When strangers misjudge their relationship, neither Christina nor Janet makes much of it, typically. But there are exceptions. "It depends how much energy we feel like exerting," says Janet. "I couldn't even tell you what the triggers are for me." But she has reacted when people park in accessible spaces without a placard. "That's not just a personal affront—it's making life harder for everybody with a disability," she explains.

Later, Janet lets me know that there may have been some who doubted the strength of their union. She doesn't say so directly, but I infer it from the way she harps on the point that certain aspects of their lives—of their personalities—are immutable and nonnegotiable. "You can't say, 'Now that Christina's disabled, you'll find some other lover,'" she says, quoting what somebody must've said to her at some point. "Well, no. That doesn't change. I love Christina. Christina *is* my lover."

As she talks, I'm reminded of when my mother told me as a child about the painter Christy Brown, made famous in the Oscar-winning movie *My Left Foot*. "He couldn't hold a paintbrush with his hand, but that didn't stop him from painting," Mom said. "He painted with the only limb he could control: his left foot." The moral: disability doesn't change who you are, or whom you love.

There's another aspect to Christina's story: chronic pain. The opioids help, but they make her brain fuzzy. And the impact on their relationship? "At bad moments of intense pain, I become removed," says Christina. "Quieter. I become so angry about the pain and the loss of control in my life that I fear if I open my mouth I'll spit fire."

I shudder at the image, but it's not entirely unfamiliar. As a rule I don't have pain, but I do seem to be uncomfortable a lot. And when I am, I know I'm downright grouchy (all right, grouchier than usual). I don't know how M.L. deals with me then or, frankly, whether she should bother trying. "What about you, Janet—how do you manage those times?"

"This is another instance where our financial resources help," comes Janet's strong voice. "Christina has a good psychotherapist she can call—somebody who isn't me to whom she can describe her pain at whatever length she wants, without it being corrosive to our relationship, without my cutting her short with, 'Yes, but can we talk about dinner now, please, honey?'" She chuckles.

I'm having trouble connecting the dots. "You're saying talk therapy helps with physical pain?"

"Yes," says Christina. "Being able to talk about it with a person who isn't in a personal or professional relationship with me but listens and keeps track—somebody who knows what I mean, who understands—"

I make a noise that lets on how surprised and fascinated I am.

"In the same way that paid care for the physical necessities helps us as a couple, the talk therapy helps keep us together," says Janet, picking up the thread of the conversation. "Both reduce the stress—physical and emotional stress."

Venting about her pain is what started Christina writing, she tells me. "It turned out I had a lot more to say than just one chapter."

In our next chat we discuss their future plans. Now that Christina is past sixty and Janet is fifty-five, they've talked with a financial advisor and estate attorney about preserving their economic resources for the long haul. Christina reminds me that Janet is now in charge of such business-minded concerns—to which Janet reacts with blunt, sobering profundity. "We're doing our best to prepare without *over*planning," says Janet. "I've learned from this whole experience that you just can't predict what's going to happen. No matter what plans you make, things will likely turn out another way."

True enough. But should I point out this is precisely *why* you're supposed to forge a financial plan, to be prepared for the unexpected? (That's my alter ego as a financial journalist weighing in.) I hold my tongue, fearing coming off preachy. Instead, what comes out of my mouth is, "How do you live with that feeling of uncertainty, of vulnerability?"

"It's a horror story!" replies Christina. "And when I contemplate aging with this quadriplegia, it frightens me to my core."

This is a good lead-in to my final line of questioning. "So," I ask, "if you could change one thing about your situation, what would it be?"

They repeat the question, mulling it over. "I'd move my job closer to Christina's," says Janet at last, "so we could live together all the time. That's what I'd do."

Christina agrees they'd prefer to live together. She's even taking a sabbatical next year, partly so they can spend more time together. There's an odd discrepancy here, though: they also cherish their boundaries. "Obviously, we've grown accustomed to having time and space apart, and we'd need that to stay built-in," says Christina. Their Middletown house, in fact, is unofficially divided into three distinct zones, she tells me. On the first floor is a wheelchair-accessible bedroom and bathroom suite they added for Christina. The upstairs is where Janet goes to "disengage." That leaves the entire downstairs living room and kitchen area for Donna, the aide. "This allows the three of us to live together pretty harmoniously," Christina says. "Of course, it's a lot more complicated in the city, where everything is so crowded."

Their apartment there is a one-bedroom measuring just 950 square feet, with a sliding wall between bedroom and living room. Sometimes the big walk-in closet doubles as a makeshift office space where Janet can go to do some work. Next year, on sabbatical, Christina figures she can always escape to Middletown—where Donna can take over custodial duties—if either one of them needs a break from the other. "I'll also be in Middletown when Janet travels for work."

Sounds complicated to me, a minefield of emotions. How will they signal when it's time for a break from each other without causing hurt feelings? I remind myself that they're used to talking through conflicts, working out disagreements with constructive dialogue. I, of all people, should know better. M.L. and I spent a couple years—when the girls were small—without any hired attendant or time apart from each other. People warned us it'd be rough, and it was, but we wanted our privacy, and we made it work.

"It's a trade-off," Christina is saying, "but we'd like more time together. Honestly, if it were possible to live together all the time, it'd enhance both of our lives."

Maybe that's the moral I've been searching for, or a part of it. Perhaps nothing else matters more than the commitment to making it work. It seems I keep coming to this conclusion: people stay together because they wish and resolve to stay together.

In the days that follow, as I review my recordings and notes, my assessment shifts somewhat. Perhaps a loving commitment can conquer all, but clearly it helps if it's armed with communication, patience, generosity, and financial resources. The lesson I glean from Christina and Janet comes in two parts: use the tools you've got, and value the process.

SIMI AND DAVID

———◆———

"IT'S A CRAZY BUSY TIME. D and I are hardly in [the] same space, except for sleeping (do u want to put that in the book?)."

This is the initial e-mail response from my friend Simi Linton when I ask about interviewing her and her husband, David. Simi is a well-known disability rights scholar and activist; David is "an able-bodied guy," as he puts it. Tooling down the streets of New York City together, they can divide crowds in spectacular fashion when he dons in-line roller skates to keep up with her motorized wheelchair. Yet the fact they're scarcely ever in the same space at the same time speaks to how independent from each other they often are. He's most definitely *not* her attendant.

Now in their late sixties, Simi and David are longtime New Yorkers who've been together some thirty-five years. I'd met them years ago, at a mutual friend's wedding, and Simi and I have exchanged occasional e-mails ever since. But I'd lost touch with David. I'd forgotten how tall, thin, and charismatic he is, with his long, wild gray hair and beard. He'd be at home in an Edward Koren cartoon in the *New Yorker*, drawn as an aging hippie or rock star in professorial glasses. The latter is fitting, since he's an emeritus professor at Marymount Manhattan College, specializing in communications and media arts.

To me, Simi seems his perfect match. She sports abundant curly auburn hair, accentuated with fashionable vintage glasses and, often, a colorful silk scarf that wreaths her Katharine Hepburn–like jaw. She's frequently decked out in bold colors—blousy tops or loose-fitting jackets with shoulder pads—and you might not even notice she's sitting in a motorized wheelchair, distracted as you might be by her sheer *oomph*. I realize I'm a tad intimidated when we finally manage to reconnect.

The warm early-spring morning of our initial chat, I'm quickly reminded she's an experienced public speaker and teacher. Years ago, Simi became an assistant professor of psychology at Baruch College and then created the Disability Studies Project at Hunter College. In 1998, in her mid-forties, she published her first book, *Claiming Disability: Knowledge and Identity*. Her second book, a memoir called *My Body Politic*, was published in 2006 and formed the basis of the documentary film *Invitation to Dance*, which Simi coproduced and codirected with Christian von Tippelskirch. It's a cinematic celebration of the physicality and grace of human movement regardless of body type or shape. Simi is now president of Disability/Arts consultancy, which she launched in 1997 to help artists and cultural institutions shape the presentation of disability in the arts and to increase the representation of work in the arts world by disabled artists.

As she describes in her memoir, Simi broke her back in a car accident in 1971 while in her early twenties. She was a sort of flower child, hitchhiking with friends and her husband at the time—John, who died in the crash—to a Vietnam War protest in Washington, DC. Afterward, in 1977, she completed a bachelor's in psychology at Columbia.

It was while she was enrolled in the PhD program at New York University, in the early 1980s, that she and David first met. "We were both in our thirties," she says in her crisp and deliberate voice. "We had both had previous marriages." (David was divorced.) "We were in different programs—" she was earning a PhD in counseling psychology, and he was getting a PhD in media studies "—but took a course in common."

From the very beginning of Simi's relationship with David, thirty-five years ago, her disability was "part of the dynamic that we grew into," David reflects, his voice both resonant and beguilingly gentle.

Simi was in a manual wheelchair then and still adjusting to her new identity as a civil-rights-minded disabled person. They came of age in their disability awareness together, David tells me. Before meeting Simi, David had had no disability experience. Listening, I'm thinking how they both speak with the forthrightness—the warmth and passion—of seasoned lecturers.

"My uncle used crutches because of childhood polio, but we were not close," he goes on. "So I'd known a few people in the community but nobody I had close proximity to or an opportunity to experience on a frequent basis."

Simi puts it this way: "David doesn't identify as disabled." As if it were a matter of choice. But I take her point: disability isn't just a functional or medical category; it's a matter of identity.

"Love at first sight?" I ask.

"Well, it was certainly a hot attraction at first sight," says David.

"So even at the start, Simi's disability wasn't an issue?"

He thinks a moment. "There were a lot of practical things to get used to," he concedes. "A lot of learning. Things like watching out for curb cuts and how to get in and out of places. There were places I would think of going spontaneously or automatically, without question, and then realize that for us to go together would be difficult or, in some cases, impossible."

Basic wheelchair access was not a given in the pre-ADA days. Simi is paraplegic, not quadriplegic; she's paralyzed from the waist down. She has good upper-body strength and, since leaving the hospital in the 1970s, has never needed personal-care assistance. Recently, however, age has taken a toll, she tells me. She now uses a motorized wheelchair because propelling a manual one became too difficult. "My shoulders no longer work the way they're supposed to," she says, her voice trailing off. I imagine she's self-correcting, wishing to go back and excise the judgmental term "supposed to" for a more neutral "used to." But then she says, "I'm not as athletic as I used to be."

I want to ask for details but decide to wait for a more opportune moment. For now, David is expanding on his introduction to architectural barriers, which foreshadows the challenges and joys to come. "Back on the question of accommodation and adjustment," he is saying, "I lived in a brownstone apartment at the time, with a steep flight of steps to get to the first floor, where I lived. When Simi came to visit, we had to figure out how she'd get into my apartment."

In her manual wheelchair, she was light enough for a strong young man to lift her up the steps—or really to bump her up a step at a time. But sometimes they'd just choose to meet elsewhere. Simi's home, of course, had no barriers.

"David seemed from early on to be open-minded and curious. That was very appealing to me."

Such traits—open-mindedness, curiosity—could be the keys to their whole marriage. Like the best teachers, they're both perpetual students. They're both open to and even eager for new experiences, new understanding. For some couples, learning about a partner's limitations and needs can be overwhelming, while for others it can be eye-opening, wondrous, intimate. Simi and David fall into the second camp. For them, the process of discovery seems to have only brought them closer.

They married in December 1981.

Learning about access barriers was just the first step (so to speak). Accessibility wasn't mandated nationally until after 1990, of course, with passage of the ADA. But before that there was a patchwork of statutes and proposals. In the 1970s and '80s, the whole country was going through a kind of consciousness-raising about reasonable accommodations and barrier removal. Besides the budding disability rights movement, there was also the start of a scholarly organization dedicated to promoting awareness of people with disabilities as a minority group, a cultural and political phenomenon rather than a medical one. I didn't hear of it till the late '80s, when the awkwardly named Section for the Study of Chronic Illness, Impairment, and Disability was mercifully redubbed the Society for Disability Studies. It's still active today, now grown to hundreds of participants around the world, publishing the *Disability Studies Quarterly* and hosting annual conferences. Simi was one of the SDS's early members.

"I kept telling David, 'This is amazing! You've got to go,'" she recalls, of those early meetings. In time she convinced him to join her. Now they're both active members.

"It was an extension of my basic curiosity," he says, "from living with her and getting involved in her perspective, her research—from just thinking about what Simi does."

As a communications professor, the hirsute scholar soon found himself participating in an SDS panel on representations of disability in popular music, followed by a panel about "interpersonal long-term romantic relationships between individuals who have disabilities and those who don't," he says.

"That's my book!" I say. "Anybody record it or take notes?"

He sighs, which I take as a no. "In the colloquial language we called it 'crip-mates,'" he goes on.

Crip-mates? I like that as a term for the able-bodied partners. But what about the crips themselves?

"I remember someone—not sure who—coined the term 'transabled love,'" interjects Simi. She sounds excited to have remembered that, but I'm thinking, *They beat me to the punch!* I'm disappointed to discover I'm venturing down an already trodden path. Still, the audience for their panel was limited, I remind myself. I also decide to stick with "interabled," since "trans" signifies a different civil rights movement these days. Curious, I ask for more details about the SDS presentation.

"I began by putting together a slideshow of clips going all the way back to Eleanor and Franklin Roosevelt," David says. "Then the four or five of us on the panel talked about our own experiences, what being in a relationship with someone with a disability was like and how that shaped the relationship, how it shaped our perspectives on ourselves."

"Is there a transcript available?" I ask again.

I detect a chuckle, as if I've asked a ridiculous question. The proceedings were fairly informal, I'm given to believe, and definitely intended for a private audience.

I ask David if he ever feels awkward or out of place at SDS conferences or in other situations where the nondisabled are in the minority, noting that my wife has experienced that phenomenon sometimes. We've never been to an SDS conference, but we've attended local disability-centric meetings. When strident activists attack the able-bodied as "the oppressive majority culture," M.L. has often felt defensive. Once, at such a meeting, a man in a wheelchair expected her to accompany him to the bathroom to empty his leg bag—without giving her a real option of declining—on the assumption that, as the only TABby in the room, she was everybody's temporary attendant. (I don't use a leg bag, and she'd never emptied one before.) After that, M.L. grew weary of these group meetings. Having a meal with a friend or two with disabilities was one thing; even driving me to and picking me up from meetings was fine. But otherwise, to this day, she prefers to remain on the periphery.

David has had a different experience. "I've been at so many SDS meetings and other settings where there's a big variety of people with a variety of disabilities that I don't feel at all alienated," he says. "But you should also know—and this may sound a little funny—I'm not generally awkward socially." He laughs, goes on to explain that he's often the first guy in the door and the last one out. Simi teases him about it, he says. She calls him "David Linton, party of one." He's just naturally outgoing. "I'm pretty engaged. It's a personality trait," he declares. "However it happens, I seem to make it clear that if you need somebody to get something for you, I'll do it. I just have a sixth sense about making things easier for people."

I can't help thinking that this sixth sense sounds awfully compatible with his role as the husband of a disabled person, and that it's something M.L. has too—a proclivity for making others' lives easier. I wonder if David's ever been asked to empty the leg bag of a woman he's just met. Doubtful, since he doesn't ordinarily do the sorts of custodial tasks M.L. does; he's probably not assumed to know how. There is also the gender bias to consider—people assume more often that women are willing to offer assistance. At any rate, David assures me that when it comes to disability-majority settings, he fits right in and enjoys them. It wasn't long, he says, before he graduated from just being "Simi's husband" to becoming accepted as an equal member of the community in his own right.

Simi abruptly interjects, "It's true for David with nondisabled people too. He bends over backward to open the door, for instance, all the time." She doesn't want me thinking he's pitying or patronizing crips, I guess. "He's just generally that way with people," she says. "It always feels quite natural to me. People look to David to do stuff because he just does it and seems comfortable with it."

As I talk with Simi and David, I'm comparing and contrasting David's characteristics with those of other "crip-mates" I've been encountering. I believe Simi is drawing an important distinction between those who are generally helpful and those who are unduly helpful with crips (if that doesn't sound too snide and ungrateful). It's a subtle distinction, perhaps, but I get it—the difference between do-gooders and extroverts, between those who need to feel needed and important and be incessantly thanked, and those who are simply socially aware and engaged. The former may never fully respect disabled people as equals, while the latter treats them as no different from anybody else. This distinction may be key. Maybe it's the binding tie that holds together the most long-lasting interabled relationships, this friendly predisposition to be of service without judgment or the expectation of much in return.

Before I can push the point, however, Simi and David are telling me about David's other disability-related involvements. He developed a college course on how disability is represented in film and television, for students of all stripes. He's been an active participant in Simi's dance initiatives, which showcase how people of all ability levels can move and swing and gesture rhythmically and elegantly—some spin on wheels or crutches, others gyrate limbs, in infinite combinations. David is in Simi's film *Invitation to Dance*. "Everybody loves to dance with him," she says. "He's danced with people with such a wide variety of impairments! And he's into it; he's curious to see how that's going to work."

That curiosity, that openness to new experiences, has proved especially helpful lately, as Simi has lost functionality. I consider now to be as good a time as any to ask about this, recognizing that disability activists generally prefer to talk about oppression and identity politics than fess up about their bodily frustrations. (Well, who wouldn't?)

But it's important to be accurate, not squeamish or sanctimonious. Simi will understand that. She'll twig that I'm not just being nosy or gossipy, right?

"You mentioned needing more help as you've gotten older," I begin, "becoming more reliant on David for certain things. Can you unpack that a bit? Give me some examples?"

"Well," she says, "David and I have had to work that out. It's been a process of working out stuff."

A sore subject? Simi has always been completely self-reliant, traveling hither and yon on her own, able to take care of herself. It must feel like a profound shift, I imagine, to no longer be able to do that. It's a new game, with new restrictions, danger zones, and rules to follow. But she seems reluctant to talk about the physical details, so I resolve to move the conversation outside the body.

"What kinds of changes have you had to make to reorganize your relationship around changing physical needs?" I say.

This time David responds. "One of the things is travel. When Simi was using a manual chair, it was easier for her to transfer into a standard car. If she was driving, she could fold her chair up and pull it into the back seat. Or if I was there, I could help fold the chair and put it in the trunk. This was especially helpful if we were traveling, renting a car. Now, however, since she's using a power chair, she can't hop into the front seat of the convertible, for instance, or into most taxis. Instead, we have a van with a ramp. There's a similar layer of complication with long-distance travel. Getting on an airplane is much harder than it used to be. Trains have become a lot more attractive because they're easier to use."

Tell me about it, I think. Story of my life. But for them, this is a recent development, a new chapter in Simi's story. It's an important point: disabilities are never static. All of us face progressions and complications, sometimes multiple complications. Our bodies betray us. Even when we feel allied with our crippled bodies, those bodies can bushwhack us.

"I'm also getting older," David reminds me. "I'm thirty-five years older than when we met, so we also have to factor in my age and changes in me and various things I've gone through. Currently I have good health, but life changes. And we have to live with that."

Yes, indeed, though a disability can accelerate one's awareness of the aging process, I muse privately.

Simi wants me to know about all the places she's traveled in the past. (Places I'll never see in person, notes a jealous voice in my head.) She's reminiscing: Japan, Hong Kong, Australia, New Zealand, Cuba, all over Europe . . . "But now I'm finding travel much more difficult," she reiterates, bringing me up short. She's as frustrated by her reality as I am by mine. Suddenly the subject of travel inaccessibility has morphed into a common thread. "The unpredictability of access and my greater needs—it's just gotten so hard," she says. *Amen!* "I'm kind of fed up with traveling! There are places I still want to go, to visit family and friends especially, but I have to really, really want to go somewhere to consider getting on a plane."

✦ ✦ ✦

Later, I'm wondering about David's role in Simi's work—expanding the presence of disability in the arts and education—and vice
versa. Is that another shared interest, another binding tie? But
the words fail me. As I look at this energetic, sharp-as-tacks couple—on whom age appears to sit as comfortably as a weathered
pair of moccasins—I'm at once envious of their apparent ease and
self-confidence, drawn in by their intelligence, and squirmy as a
little kid who's trying to wheedle more dessert.

"Do you ever feel—" I begin, then restart. "Is disability something that actually brings you closer as a couple? Or do you feel it's
a burden on your relationship? Or perhaps it's irrelevant to your
marriage? Or something else entirely?"

A pregnant pause ensues. I count the beats silently, lose track
after five.

"That's one of those questions that's nearly impossible to answer," says Simi then, "simply because this is the only way we've
known each other."

I can't help feeling I've pushed her activist buttons. It's the kind
of answer I've given people when asked, *Do you resent your disability? Do you hope for a cure? When you were a kid, didn't you want to run
and jump and play ball with the other kids?* No, no, no. I had a rich
fantasy life, sure. But who would I be without my disability? This
is the only life I've known, and I can no more imagine walking than
I can imagine flying or seeing through walls. In fact, the thought
of walking scares me because it would be so new and different. To
stand on two legs seems terrifyingly precarious, as I've informed
inquisitive strangers many times over the years.

As I've grown older, though, I can concede that it would be
nice to have a little more hand and arm strength, to be able to
cough with more force when I catch a cold. But shed my precious
wheelchair? Never! For me, disability is inborn, natural, the way
God or Mother Nature or whoever made me. If I like myself as I
am, I must also like the disability that's informed so much of who

I am and what I've become. That's the party line anyway, and I still believe it thoroughly.

But I'm asking Simi and David to talk about how they view disability. How can I make them see that what I'm trying to get at is the role of disability in a relationship? It might not be a big role, but its existence can't be denied.

Oddly, it's David who seems to grasp my point. "The question that people always want to ask me, but are usually too cautious or polite to, is whether we met before or after her injury. They don't seem to accept that, as Simi said, her disability is a given in our relationship. This is the way it's always been."

His answer resonates with me. Too often, strangers assume that my disability is a recent development and that M.L. has "stuck by me" out of some noble obligation. That's why I've put our wedding photo front and center in our home, in hopes that anyone who crosses our threshold won't ask such stupid questions.

"You could ask any disabled person, 'How central is disability in your life?'" says Simi. "Well, if they found a cure tomorrow, I'd be out of a career." This echoes something I might've uttered. My financial journalism pays the bills, but my disability-related writing is my career. She goes on to tell me that disability is an essential part of her life, that the world defines her as a disabled person and that it's part of her public and private identity. All her work and thinking and life are wrapped around her identity as a person with a disability. "And the environment—both social-cultural and physical—is such that I'm constantly reminded I'm a disabled person in a world that's not designed for people like me."

I smile, digging her wisdom, though her response doesn't fully answer my query. To be sure, disability isn't just about barriers and needs. It's a characteristic, a marker that impacts how you see yourself and how others see you. But what about the way it's affected their personal home life? I say: "So in your relationship—?"

"It's very much central to our relationship," says Simi, "for all those reasons. Apart from how we may feel about my disability, it's central to us as a couple." It's also central to their social life, she goes on. She estimates half their close friends have disabilities. That wasn't the case when they were newlyweds. "I was much newer to the disability game then," she says, "not as clearly identified as I am now. My work was sort of there early on, but I've grown into it professionally."

Grown into her disability. I like that—a good lesson there about adjusting, about assimilating all of one's traits into a mature sense of self. Yet I still feel misunderstood, so I reiterate my premise: my disability, I say, assumed by many to be a burden, may actually enhance the intimacy of my marriage. M.L. and I have perhaps fewer illusions about each other than other couples seem to and are more in touch with each other's limitations and needs than we might otherwise be. "Have you two ever felt that way?"

David answers: "Here's one thing that maybe relates to what you're saying. When we met, I was already politically inclined, but my sense of justice and equality—my sense of the role that society plays in shaping our lives and experiences—has been strongly enhanced by my relationship with Simi. She's given me a deeper way of looking at the culture and society—at other people's formulations and values, at prejudices and unnecessary restrictions. That's been a tremendous enhancement to my political and social breadth! I see things I wouldn't otherwise have seen, and that's been a deeply enriching experience for me."

I'll take that. In an interabled marriage—or in any mixed marriage—you learn about a world, a subculture, quite different from the one you grew up in. For M.L. and me, she's learned about Reform Judaism as much as about disabilities, just as I've learned about Congregationalism. It's the old lesson drummed into educators and human resources professionals and politicians everywhere: diversity enriches us all.

But to me there's another inference: certain types of people are more open to that kind of enrichment than others. If you're lucky enough to be married to one of them, and you're in an interabled or any other kind of mixed marriage, your chances of long-lasting success seem greater. On the other hand, if disability enters the marriage later, by surprise, I guess you'll find out pretty quickly how open you are to that kind of enrichment.

My conversations with the Lintons have led me to consider that the presence of openness may cement the connection in some interabled couples, just as its absence may tear others apart.

COLLEEN AND MAX

—◆—

ONE MORNING I HEAR an interview on NPR that stops me cold. It's a woman talking fondly about her long interabled marriage, though she doesn't use that term. I go online to look up her name: Colleen Kelly Starkloff. I haven't heard of her, but I track her down. A widow, she has a particular perspective about which I want to know more. Call it the long view. I'm delighted when she agrees to chat.

"I was a physical therapist," she explains to me, her voice rising for emphasis. "All the paraplegics and quadriplegics I saw were skinny and hanging on for dear life. They didn't know where they were going with their lives after rehab."

Sixty-five-years old when we first talk, she was married for thirty-five years to Max Starkloff, a longtime disability rights advocate. Their marriage ended in December 2010 with his death at seventy-three. Max was a C3–C5 quad from a 1959 car accident at twenty-one. Does she have any regrets about their time together? Sure, nobody speaks ill of the dead. But I figure she has nothing to lose now by answering honestly.

From her office in St. Louis, Colleen is reminiscing about 1973, when she was the twenty-three-year-old director of physical therapy at St. Joseph's Hill, a Franciscan nursing home about forty miles from where she is today. She remains tall, slender, and fit, though she no longer sports the long brown hair I see in photos from that time. It's not hard to imagine her, at nineteen, as the hometown beauty-pageant contestant she was.

But her description of her rehab patients back then as "skinny and hanging on for dear life" takes me aback. It could be offensive—except it's coming from her. I wait silently. She has a bigger point to make.

"It's interesting," she muses, changing tone, pausing to conjure memories. "I don't know how many PTs go home at night thinking about the kinds of things I thought about—things like, what did you do today to make somebody's life better? Maybe you taught someone to put their pants on or lift five pounds with a weight strapped around their wrist. Valuable skills, but what are you rehabilitating them for? That's what I began to think about. What world are they going back into? Is it a world where they can ride the bus, get a job, get married, have kids? What are they going to do after they get out of the institution?"

The institution is where she met Max. He was thirty-five then, twelve years her senior and fourteen years into his quadriplegia, most of which time he'd lived at St. Joseph's. He was a big man, six feet five inches tall and nearly two hundred fifty pounds, unable to feel or move a muscle from the chest down. His mother had institutionalized him reluctantly, only after finding she couldn't provide what he needed and keep her job. His father had abandoned the family years earlier.

"When I first met Max, I fell in love immediately," recalls Colleen. "I had dated a lot of young men, but none of them seemed to have a sense of purpose. Max did. That was what really attracted me to him. I looked in his eyes, and I just saw something I hadn't seen in anybody else. The quality of who he was came through in his eyes."

She had already heard his name from her sister, Mary, who also worked there. Max had asked Mary out first, and she'd refused, "because he's disabled," Colleen reports. Which didn't matter to Colleen.

"His disability wasn't a factor for me," she says.

Soon she was visiting him in his claustrophobic institutional room twice a day, before and after work.

"He was never my patient," she stresses. "We'd just sit and talk."

Max had a lot to talk about. He'd begun exploring ways to get out of the nursing home, to create opportunities for himself and others like him. In the biography *Max Starkloff and the Fight for Disability Rights*, by Charles E. Claggett Jr. and Richard H. Weiss, Colleen is quoted as saying,

> It was in those conversations that I began to learn about people with disabilities' being institutionalized. Until that time, I had only seen the rehabilitation side of disabilities, the side where we help them to get out into the community. Now I was seeing that there was this whole other side . . . from the perspective of the disabled people. And I was absolutely fascinated by it and by the fact that Max really wanted to do something about it. And I wanted to help him do something about it.

Soon their conversation moved from getting people out of institutions to going out on a date. Thanks partly to donations from friends, Max had purchased an old VW van with a makeshift wheelchair ramp. Colleen drove. He had to be back in his room at the institution by seven thirty, though, so the staff could get him into bed. Later they took to having dinner together in his room—simple meals she'd prepare there, on an electric burner. She'd leave the room when the attendant came to put him to bed, then return to continue talking until lights out.

Hearing the details of their story, I'm secretly slightly aroused by the hot glow of clandestine romance all linked up with big ideas, the sharing of deep-seated political thoughts and dreams. "The personal is political," the feminist pioneer Carol Hanisch said. This was certainly true for the Starkloffs. Colleen began driving Max to meetings of the National Paraplegia Foundation, where they met other progressive thinkers in the fledgling disability rights movement, further bonding them to each other. Colleen says she changed from having a conservative Republican view to a "more liberal Democratic" one because the Republicans she spoke to didn't seem to share her concerns about the rights of people with disabilities.

Soon Colleen was assisting Max in all his political activities, typing letters and grant proposals, making phone calls, and driving to events. But make no mistake: their alliance was also romantic. On New Year's Eve 1973 they went to a party together and ended up snowed in. For the first time, she lifted Max out of his wheelchair into bed—she knew how because of her PT training—and for the first time, they slept together.

I ask her how others reacted to their union. "People did tell Max things like, 'You're so lucky to have found somebody willing to have you,'" Colleen responds. "And I constantly had to deal with the old, 'He's so lucky he has you'—meaning he was lucky to have someone *to take care of him.*" You can hear the scoffing, bitter irony in her voice. "I don't believe in this nonsense of having to take care of disabled people. It diminishes their ability to figure out ways of taking care of themselves. It betrays a lack of understanding about what's really going on."

I agree, "caregiving" is an icky, patronizing term, but let's face it—wasn't caregiving what was going on?

Colleen acknowledges that, throughout their marriage, she was Max's primary attendant. She prefers to say she worked for him as a "personal assistant," excising the word "care," which, she says, "suggests that the disabled person cannot take care of him/herself. That's a slippery slope. . . . Max took care of himself by making decisions about what would and would not take place in his daily routines—and by extension, what would and would not take place in his life."

But some degree of care was involved, right?

Only in the affectionate sense, she insists. "It was love," she says. "If you love somebody, you love them for who they are and not what issues they bring."

I revisit the question in our second conversation. I know that activists sometimes respond with facile, even rehearsed responses, and I want to examine this further: what underlies providing personal assistance for a spouse? If you can't manage it—physically, emotionally, financially, whatever—does that mean you don't have enough love? Surely not. Do you have to be a self-sacrificing type to make such a situation work? Perhaps Colleen is forgetting how hard she had to work as an attendant/wife/mother.

She lets out a knowing chuckle. "I was canonized many times!"

"But how did you react?" I ask.

"Depends on the situation. Typically I'd say something like, 'Well, I got the better part of the deal. You should know him! We are a team and work together on almost everything we do.' Sometimes I'd add, 'I'm very proud to be his wife.'" A pause. A deep breath. "I do get that people mean well, but to canonize me as if something beyond love—mutual love—was going on, just because I married a disabled guy, demeans Max and others with disabilities. I can't abide that."

Back in 1973, as a recent graduate of St. Louis University and a fledgling PT, Colleen Kelly had to face much worse. Friends hassled her about why she was dating "this handicapped guy," she says. Her own parents thought she was being unrealistic and told her so. This may have only made her all the more determined. In June 1975 Max proposed to her, and she accepted immediately.

That October, the day before the wedding, Max was released from St. Joseph's. He was thirty-eight. He had lived in the institution for twelve years. Funded partly by a friend's donation, they rented a small apartment at first, ultimately buying a fixer-upper house they renovated for accessibility.

She knew they might not be able to have kids the old-fashioned way, but she figured, *So what? We'll adopt.* She knew that quads weren't considered employable and that they were prone to pressure sores, bladder infections, and a host of other maladies, but she didn't care. Everybody takes risks, she'd argue, especially when they fall in love.

Together, they organized a coalition of civic leaders and charitable contributions to build Max's dream: Paraquad. Originally conceived of as an accessible residential complex where people with and without disabilities could live, work, and shop, Paraquad instead became one of the nation's premier centers for independent living—a nonresidential community organization controlled by people with disabilities for people with disabilities (the residential aspects were dropped after numerous complications arose). Specifically, Paraquad helps crips in the St. Louis area find attendants, secure government benefits to which they're entitled, and trains them to advocate for themselves and secure a more independent lifestyle than most had known before. (Later, in 1982, Max helped launch the National Council on Independent Living, which still serves, advocates for, and coordinates the efforts of organizations similar to Paraquad across the United States.)

Today Colleen calls her former life as a PT "sitting on a mat with somebody, which was boring." She doesn't mince words. She is a natural advocate and so forthright that I want to joke, "So how do you really feel about it?"

"For me, a man like Max was easy to love, because I value people of passion and compassion and commitment," she says. "He was driven by not only 'I'm going to get out of here'"— meaning the nursing home—"but 'I'm taking you with me.' And he stuck with that and made it happen. People who are committed to making the world better are wonderfully strong, interesting, and fascinating. That quality, that was something I could wrap myself around."

I'm reminded of how Alison Hockenberry explained her early attraction to John, the appeal of a man who is bold and independent. Yet surely Max and Colleen had private moments of despair or strife?

"It got stormy sometimes," she allows. "We were two very strong personalities. I remember within the first year of our marriage, I once took off my wedding ring—it probably cost all of two hundred bucks, but it was precious to me—and threw it across the living room because I was so mad at him. I don't remember why. He was huffy too, and we didn't speak to each other for a while. But by that night when we went to bed, we were apologizing."

I wonder if they had to make peace because she was his attendant. Apologize, or no bed for you. She's not buying it.

"Even if we weren't speaking to each other for days on end, it wasn't like I was not going to get him in and out of bed or do what he needed. To me that would've been hitting below the belt."

In the Claggett and Weiss biography, Max is described as charismatic, a natural salesman who in his youth before the accident had many girlfriends. I wonder if he used that charm to make sure his needs were met.

"Max never had to pressure me," Colleen holds. "He had a real sense of pride. He wouldn't give in without a fight, but if we had a disagreement, we both made a point of fighting fair." When pressed, she acknowledges there were times when she wondered if she could keep executing the tasks of his personal assistant. "Was I going to have to keep lifting a man who weighed more than two hundred pounds in and out of his chair, to and from bed, every day for the rest of my life? But I did it. I did until the day he died," she says.

"But at times you must've felt a certain pressure," I say. "Everything depended on your ability, no?"

"I wouldn't use the word 'pressure,'" she answers, "because it was part of my marital agreement. For me it was, I've got to keep doing it so I can continue to do it and not lose my ability to do it. Getting him in and out of bed was just a part of my day. And I figured if there came a time when I could no longer do that, we'd just hire attendants."

✦   ✦   ✦

One area of strife for them, however, involved children. He wasn't so sure he wanted to have any, perhaps because he wasn't able to procreate in the old-fashioned way, perhaps because he feared the additional drain on time, energy, money, and other finite resources he depended on. Colleen, on the other hand, had a strong maternal urge.

"I was the oldest of twelve kids! I practically grew up helping take care of my younger siblings," she says. "I can't explain the nurturing issue that I feel, but it's there, you know? And I couldn't explain my desire to be a mother to a man who didn't get it. That was a big bone of contention, but he finally gave in."

Actually, within months of their wedding she was calling adoption agencies. She was told they had to have been married for at least five years to receive due consideration. (In time, they also tried artificial insemination, but it didn't work.) So in 1980 she put in new adoption applications. One agency turned them down because Max couldn't play ball with a child, she recalls. Another said no because Max would probably die at a young age. Nevertheless, she persisted (to quote a phrase). The couple had become prominent members of the community by then, through their disability advocacy—mingling with politicians and corporate leaders. By the end of 1980 they finally found a willing agency. They adopted a baby girl they named Meaghan. Six years later they adopted a boy they named Max, and in 1989 came Emily.

Colleen handled all the physical tasks of parenting, while Max provided strong emotional support in the form of love and encouragement but also discipline. "He adored all three of them," says Colleen.

In time, they hired part-time attendants so Colleen didn't have to assist Max all the time while looking after the kids.

"We did have attendants for the last fifteen years or so, but they weren't full-time," she says. "The attendants just helped with getting up in the morning and going to bed at night. And they only worked five days a week. So I still had two days a week. That wasn't just to save money. I wanted to keep doing it so I wouldn't get out of practice and become unable to do it." (They also had a sort of jury-rigged lifting device, but it wasn't portable. So manual transfers to and from bed remained the norm.)

Still, even when there was hired help, Colleen was the go-to assistant for holidays and traveling. "If we got on a plane, I would never let anybody touch him. I didn't want anybody to drop him," she says. "Max would say, 'Let the airline people help with the transfer, Sweetie,' and I would tell him, 'Look at those knuckle-heads! They're knuckle-draggers, and they don't know how to lift people. If something happens to you, we could be paying for it for a really long time. I think it's better if you let me, don't you?' And he'd say, 'Yes, you're right.'"

Her protectiveness reminds me of M.L.'s idea that if she doesn't provide the assistance, it won't get done right. It's true, in most cases, even if it sometimes feels intrusive or overprotective. I've always preferred to maintain full-time paid assistance, if possible. I need it for my sense of control, of autonomy. Plus, I feel M.L. needs it for her own sense of independence and freedom. Colleen talks as if she was perfectly content devoting her life to Max's. I wonder if her attitude was affected by the generational expectations for wives.

"I knew what I was getting into from the beginning," she says. "I knew what was involved in getting him up every day. I knew the most personal details of it. And it was like, okay, that's not a deal breaker for me at all. It's something you learn to do, and then you just do it. It becomes part of your day. I never had a problem with that."

I'm so dubious of her insistence that she never felt constrained by the pressures of her marriage that I revisit the point several weeks later. I think of the many meals M.L. and I have had when her attention is drawn away by our kids or, more recently, an alert from her cell phone. I get mad because I'm still hungry and need her to feed me, but she's distracted. Then again, I know she's already been feeding me for an hour, has finished her own dinner, and is justified in being antsy or needing a break.

At other times, M.L. has admitted to fantasizing about running away from it all, chucking the responsibilities of motherhood and wifehood, let alone of being the ever-on-call backup attendant. "We could arrange for you to take a vacation for a couple days. Just you, by yourself," I've suggested.

"I'm afraid," she once told me, "if I went away for any length of time, I might never come back."

When M.L.'s father was dying, we did arrange for her to visit him in Seattle. She was away just three or four days. I arranged for an attendant to sleep over, and our teenage niece helped with the girls, who were still small. Afterward, M.L. told me how great it felt, despite the sad occasion, to rent a car at SeaTac and just drive on her own. It gave her a sense of recapturing her youth. But she did return, of course, and we went on as we had before.

Didn't Colleen and Max ever get into conundrums like these, volatile moments of competing needs?

"I believed he could take care of himself and our children if anything were to happen to me," Colleen tells me in our next interview. "He would do that by making decisions about who/what/where would need to be done if something took me out of the picture. That actually played out when I got sick with the flu a few times. I was too sick to take care of the kids, fix dinner, get him up, etc. He took over and made decisions and phone calls and—*bada bing, bada boom*—all I had to do was lie in bed and be sick. He took care of me and the kids and got someone else to get him up. He had a driver to get the kids to school and himself to work. He did not drive. In so doing, Max took care of himself and the others in his life."

I'm growing envious. I think I've got this disability thing down to a science—M.L. and I together—but Colleen is making her long marriage to Max sound golden. I wonder if I carry off the inner strength, the sense of self-reliance, that Max apparently had. I'm keeping score, I realize too late. I'm losing perspective. After all, I remind myself, these are the reminiscences of a widow wearing rose-colored glasses.

"I never felt trapped," she is telling me. "When I did take a few trips to spend a week with a close friend—I took the kids with me, to make it easier for Max to concentrate on work and himself—I couldn't wait to get back. . . . I missed him terribly when we were apart." Which was rare, she concedes. They worked together, in separate offices but in the same building. "He would call me several times a day," she says.

In time, they were able to buy a second home in Innsbrook, about sixty miles east of St. Louis.

"It gave us time away from the phone and the Movement, to just spend with our kids and friends," she says. "We all loved it, and I find Max there even now. I go most weekends. . . ." She trails off.

At Innsbrook, she'd go horseback riding while Max watched the kids swim, fish, or go canoeing in the lake.

"He'd teach the kids how to play baseball. He was the umpire, of course. He also told them stories or supervised them building forts out of boxes. . . . Max had a great imagination, and he encouraged the kids to develop theirs too."

That *is* something I can relate to.

Then, in 2007, at sixty-nine years old, Max fell out of his wheelchair and punctured a lung. A full-time tracheotomy and ventilator followed.

In recovery, he could no longer be alone. It also became harder to do basic custodial tasks for him. Getting him up in the morning used to take a little more than an hour, but after the punctured lung, it took two and a half hours. More paid attendants were needed.

Hearing this, I flash back to my own hospitalization circa 2007–2008. I managed to wean myself off the ventilator, at least for the time being, though I still have the trach. I knew that in my new postoperative state I'd have to look for a more skilled level of assistance than I was used to. I'd have to pay more than pennies over minimum wage. No question that the more you pay, the better the employee, though that's no guarantee. (I believe in raising the minimum wage to support a decent standard of living, but I can't deny that wage inflation hurts me and others like me who have to pay for help out of our own pockets. To get an adequate pool of attendants, I have to pay double McDonald's wages.)

Nevertheless, my life did get back to normal after my hospitalization, more or less. In fact, the experience became a kind of jump-start, a rebirth. For Max, I'm told, the accident greatly diminished his energies. But that's not what ultimately defeated him.

In May 2008, Colleen and Max's youngest child, Emily, nineteen, was killed by a hit-and-run driver. She was intending to become a nurse and had reportedly learned to do her father's suctioning—the insertion of a small tube into the trach to vacuum out gunk from the lungs, something I've never had the courage to teach my children to do.

"It was a tragedy for us, needless to say," says Colleen. "But being together, holding on to each other, enabled us to get through. I don't even know what words to use to talk about it."

Max fell into a deep depression. Had he lived long enough, who knows if he would've risen out of it? But on December 27, 2010, at seventy-three, he succumbed to complications from the flu.

Looking back, Colleen clearly has no regrets. "We were hugely happy in our life together," she says. "Max and I were committed to the same work and to building a family together. We did those things pretty much in harmony. We knew how each other thought. And even when we disagreed, we would listen to each other's views."

As Max became a prominent personality in the disability rights movement, Colleen knew her views were playing second fiddle. Yet in retrospect she betrays no resentment. "I was proud of Max—always. I did work to promote him. We also both had big egos, so sometimes there was friction when an idea I had didn't make the cut. But that was my ego getting in my own way. He typically trumped my ideas, but I learned from him and his ideas and his actions."

This wasn't just 1950s-era wifely submissiveness. What she learned was how to be a disability rights advocate. Even to this day, more than five years after Max's death, Colleen still runs his final legacy project, the Starkloff Disability Institute, which is a kind of think tank devoted to the employment of people with disabilities. In other words, at sixty-six years old, she's still in the disabilities business.

"Absolutely!" she says. "It's my passion. It's all I know. I wouldn't feel fulfilled doing anything else."

Months go by before I get in touch with Colleen again. I want her to sign a consent form to use her story in this book. She's game, but she has a concern. "I see why you want to use the title *In Sickness and in Health*, but Max and I never considered disability about being sick. It sends the wrong message, in our view, about living with disability."

I tell her that I have had misgivings about the title myself. My own disability is from a congenital circumstance I don't consider an illness, although many other disabilities are certainly caused by injuries and/or illnesses. Nevertheless, I say, the proposed title does seem to get the message across and is easily understood by a vast number of readers.

She says she understands but elaborates on her view. "We've spent our careers working to change societal attitudes on the part of nondisabled people toward people with disabilities [away] from viewing us as sick to viewing us as people just like everyone else, except that we've had to deal with disability—which, when successfully done, makes one very powerful and strong."

I'm not totally comfortable with separating "us disabled people" from "those sick people." They're people too, after all, and we do have a lot in common. But I don't say any of this to Colleen. She makes a good point.

Colleen goes on to tell me she was recently in an accident and broke her hip so severely "the surgeon wanted me to stay home for *two months*," she says, which was too long. The doctor was concerned about her bearing weight on the leg before it healed. She couldn't bear to stay bedridden that long and came up with an alternate plan. "I had a few secret weapons!" she says. "I have Max's wheelchair, his van with a lift, [and an] accessible home and second home. I also work in [an] accessible office. So I asked the surgeon to let me go back to work after just three weeks. He was also Max's surgeon and knew what we stand for. He immediately understood that if I'm in Max's power chair I can easily get around plus be non-weight-bearing. So he agreed to let me start back to work and my regular life!"

Then something even more profound happened. Living in a chair for more than a month gave her a new understanding of the disability experience.

"[It] allowed me to see even better why chair-users wheel in the street," she says, referring to the fact that many of us avoid crowded, potholed sidewalks, especially if the curbs at crosswalks aren't ramped, "[and] fret about ruts in the lips on curb cuts." (When rolling up or down a ramped curb, a crack or bump in the sidewalk can easily catch a wheelchair's small front or rear casters, potentially causing the chair to capsize or get stuck in place.) She has a new appreciation for architectural accessibility, she says—all the things "we've fought for over the past forty-plus years." Besides curb cuts, she cites lifts on buses, level entrances on trains, accessible thresholds into and within buildings. "We certainly aren't at the finish line yet, but what a change from when Max and I started our work to pursue a world that welcomes all people with disabilities!"

Beyond giving her a renewed firsthand sense of what underlies the cause that's dominated her life, the experience has rekindled her romantic memories as well.

"Many times over these past few weeks I've thought how Max still takes care of me even now. He taught me how to live with dignity and with disability, albeit temporary. [In his wheelchair] I can go wherever I want to go." And that, she says, makes her "the luckiest woman on the planet for having had Max in my life for thirty-seven years. I miss him still and will for the rest of my life."

To have gained so much from her lengthy interabled romance, she clearly had an enduring intimacy that anyone would envy. There's a message in their example that could, I hope, help insecure interabled newbies as much as it could alter common perceptions of life's possibilities for those with disabilities. Yet I know too that however sincere her words, Colleen is an activist set on making a point—an activist whose views are surely tinged with nostalgia. That's not necessarily a bad thing, though, is it?

CONCLUSION

ON THAT HUMID NIGHT IN STAMFORD, Connecticut, more than three decades ago when M.L. and I started our relationship, we may not have expected it to last. But as the pace of our passion downshifted from summer lust to something more measured but equally, even more deeply felt, we found we couldn't live without each other—and ultimately moved in together and then drove across country together and became engaged and, eventually, married.

Through most of that time, we naïvely believed love would conquer all. We weren't wrong exactly, but it's clear now—after talking to so many other long-lasting couples—that credit is also due to stubbornness, open-mindedness, creative problem-solving, conscientious communication, ingenuity, luck, financial support, patience, and a monumental revolution in legal and cultural attitudes toward people who are marginalized, who are deemed different.

I started this project hoping to gain knowledge about how unusual my marriage is and about what mechanisms or elements have kept us going. I end it with a deeper appreciation for what is "normal" about M.L. and me and what is exceptional. We've always been good partners, but as in any partnership there have been extended rough patches. For instance, in the early years (yes, alas, it was a matter of years), to test my attractiveness, I used to flirt with other women with abandon—waitresses, strangers in online chat rooms, just about any and all female friends. I never really expected these dalliances to lead anywhere—and whenever it seemed as if one might, I'd abruptly pull back and insert the words "my girlfriend" (or "fiancée" or "wife") into the conversation to end the innuendo. I simply needed to be sure that there could've been others and that I was part of this union by choice, not out of fear or necessity. As intelligent, beautiful, sexy, companionable, compassionate, competent, funny, and feisty as M.L. is—and as compatible as we may be in interests, tastes, values—I *had* to know.

I should've known better. Now I do.

M.L. tolerated my flirting—she didn't like it, but she trusted me, she said—even if she didn't totally understand it. "As long as no one gets hurt," she'd say (in memory, she'd fold her arms while uttering these words, like the schoolteacher she was then). I confess, I sometimes wished she'd act a little more jealous. "I liked living on my own, before you," she told me recently. "When I realized you were the one person I wanted to give that up for, I knew you had to be the one."

Same here. It just took me a little longer to believe it. (Forgive me, please, my foolish, childish insecurities.)

I also reflect back on the support group M.L. and I tried to form more than twenty years ago. The idea was to get interabled couples together to talk about their issues. But neither of us knew how to run a group. The bigger problem, however, was that some folks showed up to kvetch and garner sympathy while others had political axes to grind. Heated arguments ensued, and insults flew like collateral shrapnel. If there was any common ground among these couples, it was purely superficial.

The lesson I took away from this failed experiment was that even among the population of interabled couples, there were vast differences. It shouldn't have surprised me, really. I knew all too well—have always known—that my disability doesn't define who I am. Why should a disability define a romantic union?

There's a similar takeaway from this book. From the couples I interviewed and others I've known, I can see that all relationships—whether interabled or not—face a particular set of challenges and rely on a certain set of strengths. If that seems obvious to you, it wasn't always obvious to me. But maybe, if I'd thought about it, I should've known it going in.

I do believe I've learned a few tips from the conversations captured here. Not life-changing, soul-nourishing, Sermon on the Mount quality wisdom, perhaps, but profoundly simple truths. The biggest of these might be that disability makes a convenient scapegoat. Snags will happen inevitably, but you can't blame all the difficulties on the disability. Maybe none of them. You need to have a kind of raw, bred-in-the-bone clarity about where to place the fault when times are tough (hint: it's probably not with the disability itself, but with outside forces that fail to accommodate it).

Recognizing this together, as a couple—sharing in this wisdom—can not only lead to more effective solution-finding but, I suspect, make interabled partnerships uncommonly intimate and enduring.

I also end this exploration realizing something else I might've gleaned from the beginning: coupling isn't just about finding happiness. While committed partners pool resources, share quotidian chores and responsibilities, bolster each other's egos, and support each other in old age, they are also frequently moved to perpetuate the species. It's sometimes given as the primary reason for getting married, the desire for children. Couples in which disability factors in are no exception.

M.L. and I have always been able to listen to each other, respect each other's strengths, and not (often) insult each other's weaknesses, and these values have been inculcated in our offspring. Our consideration for each other, our insistence that problems can be worked out, and whatever else we've managed to do to maintain and grow our relationship have been passed down as well. In our family of four, there are always competing requirements and requests vying for priority. Taking turns becomes essential. Each of us must try to be patient, though we don't always succeed at it. We often have to wait for or improvise around getting the help or attention or privacy we crave. Perhaps every family does. But somehow—maybe partly because of my disability—we're habituated to acknowledging limitations and needs. None of us really expects to have it all. I like to think we're also used to the idea of fairness.

Our kids have, I believe, learned patience, compassion, tolerance, and a sense of pride. They've learned they have the capacity to help others without looking down on them and to make a difference in the world. Check this out: for a school assignment several years ago, my elder daughter—now in her early twenties—wrote about what it was like growing up with a physically disabled parent.

> I vividly recall the pride I felt helping my dad adjust the position of his hand on his wheelchair controller on a busy street corner. "Not every 3-year-old can be trusted to do this," I thought. My dad has spinal muscular atrophy. . . .
>
> The basic realities of having a physically disabled parent have affected who I am in meaningful ways and made me a more thoughtful and independent person.
>
> I started to take responsibility for fulfilling my own needs at a young age. The point at which a child is no longer the one who needs the most help with basic tasks usually comes with the birth of a little sibling. For me, it came as soon as I was able to raise a spoon to my mouth more effectively than my quadriplegic father. This instilled in me the knowledge that often the most pressing need is not my own. It also taught me, however, the importance of asking for help when I need it. My dad has shown me that there is nothing wrong with asking for what you need, and his fight for reasonable accommodations often helps others who need the same things.
>
> In fact, it's amazing how often my dad needs to ask for basic accessibility. . . . My dad has shown me how to be aware of ways

in which a world that functions fine for me might not for others. . . . Growing up with my dad has taught me to see beyond my own point of view and not let "not my problem" excuse me from finding a solution.

I guess we didn't do so badly as parents, M.L. and I.

In no way am I claiming we're an ideal family. Far from it. But once you've had your kids help straighten you up in your wheelchair or drive it down the street when your hand gives out, you tend to reevaluate your perception of propriety and family roles.

Just as my firstborn gained an early sense of self-confidence and responsibility from helping me, I was being carried to a place of humble appreciation. Getting her help in this intimate way didn't diminish my essential *daddiness*, as I'd feared. She still needed me to be her dad—still does—but in terms we defined and finagled on our own.

I recall one summer evening during a family vacation. My firstborn—she couldn't have been more than seven at the time—was sitting on my lap, and she drove us in my wheelchair down the streets of midtown Manhattan to a neighborhood bodega, where we purchased a small chocolate cake. She had to hand the cashier money from my wallet and collect the change; I talked her through it. Afterward, she was so proud and couldn't wait to share the cake with M.L., who'd stayed in our hotel suite to nurse the baby to sleep. This became a high point of the trip! My daughter still talks fondly about it and other, similar adventures. (We explored art galleries, water fountains, vending machines, "hidden" courtyards, and so forth.) Altogether, they make up a particular kind of father-daughter bonding.

Whenever I feel guilty about how independent and self-sufficient my kids have had to be because of my disability, or because M.L. is helping me and can't always help them, I think back further, to my own childhood. In my high school years, I spent many evenings alone at home with my attendant while my divorced mother went out with her gentleman friend. How I loved those evenings! I felt so grown up, never considering as I ate the dinner my mother had laid up for me the thousand invisible support systems at work propping up my seeming autonomy. I knew it wasn't a conventional childhood, and that's partly why I liked it.

Perhaps my kids feel the same way about theirs.

In all the conversations in this book, I've made a point of never sugarcoating the sometimes bitter realities. These aren't all cheery stories with happy endings. Rather, they're as promised—conversations about love, disability, and the perils and pleasures of interabled couplings—the good experiences and the bad.

During my research, I came to see how different the world is today for young people with disabilities. I came away convinced that if I were a young man today, even with the advanced extent of my disabilities, I wouldn't be doomed to loneliness and isolation. I'd probably use the Internet to meet people and find love; many young people now do seem receptive to the idea of disabled people as potential romantic—even sexual—partners, even if some need a little seducing. So different from when I was young! Finding a lasting partner when you have disabilities is still not easy, even in the twenty-first century, but then little worth having is.

I also came to appreciate the importance of families to the success of interabled couples. Without their support, emotional and financial, it can be much harder for romance to blossom and mature. Whether or not to have children is still a daunting question for these couples (as it is for many others), but even those who faced parenting challenges have few if any regrets—sometimes as much to their own disbelief as to outsiders'.

Without exception, all the people I interviewed face unwelcome comments from strangers—even if well-intentioned, they may lead couples to question their place in the world. Some are more bothered by unpleasant remarks than others, but all, I think, gain strength from defying the negative vibes that surround them. Damn the naysayers!

What's most surprising is that few of the people in this book have any regrets or unmet desires at all. Sure, everyone wishes for more creature comforts—money, primarily. But no one told me, *If only we had an accessible van, I could go places*, or *What I could really use is easier access to health care*, or *We'd be so happy if we just had more freedom from (a) our families, (b) terrible personal-care assistants, (c) each other.* Maybe they didn't want to admit such deeply personal complaints to me. Or maybe they're so used to filling (or circumventing) the holes in their lives that they don't think twice about them. The daily problems become manageable nuisances.

I have tried to meet romantic pairings in a broad spectrum of situations—a mix of old friends and strangers, of familiar diagnoses and some I'd never heard of. Yes, I've been drawn to wheelchair users rather than those with other types of disabilities, because that's what I am: a wheelchair user. But there are a lot of different situations. And with a tremendous sense of relief and enlightenment, I've also found that many of the experiences these couples have are universal—such as concerns about money and worries about the future.

Frankly, I'm loath to draw any generalities. There are no rules of attraction. Interabled romance cuts across all socioeconomic, political, religious, racial, gender, gender-orientation, gender-identity, and other potentially divisive lines. Indeed, it may help draw people together across these potential divides. I found no truth in the broad assumption that it's easier for disabled men to find able-bodied partners than it is for disabled women. Similarly, those of us with congenital disabilities may not know the trauma of those who acquire them later in life, but that doesn't necessarily mean our romantic lives are any easier or harder.

True, those with disabilities often struggle to feel respected as valid, sensible, independent adults and true romantic partners. Yet, later, when initial hesitancies about exposing our most intimate details to our partners dissipate, we feel bound by a profound sense of trust, of give-and-take. We may be unsure about how we'll keep up as we age, but we're confident in the strength and longevity of our relationships.

Given how easy it's been to find willing volunteers for my research and how many I've had to turn away to avoid redundancy, this process has reassured me that M.L. and I aren't exactly an extraordinary phenomenon. If we differ from other couples in some ways, it's solely because of specific elements in our personalities and lifestyle choices.

One of the couples whose story I couldn't include here involves a woman with SMA and her live-in attendant, also her longtime lover. Their tale was similar to others', except for one salient fact: they're not legally married. "In our eyes, we're married," she told me. "To everyone else, unfortunately, we're simply roommates." Like same-sex couples in the bad old days, they had a small private commitment ceremony but couldn't officially wed for fear that the partner with SMA would lose her government benefits. Since I'd already covered the marriage penalty for people with disabilities who rely on government benefits, I decided theirs was a story I'd already told.

A young African American woman who's married to a white man who uses a wheelchair wrote to say that the interracial element of their relationship "adds an additional flavor [and] set of stereotypes. . . . An able-bodied black woman in the presence of a white guy in a wheelchair must obviously be the hired help!" At restaurants, in stores, at movies, on public transit, or even at the hospital, she says, "I don't encounter surprise that we are a couple as much as I encounter the assumption we are not."

I know the feeling. I think everyone profiled here does, no matter their race or other physical characteristics. How often is my wife taken to be my nurse or my sister or even, once, my mother! And we're more or less the same color, she and I.

Then there was the young man with no legs who uses a wheelchair and his fiancée who's hearing impaired. Though I liked their story, double-disability duos—of which there are many—were beyond the scope of this work.

✦ ✦ ✦

I think now that it may be at our most stressed moments that M.L. and I feel closest. Like when a nation is at war and all sorts of different interests band together toward a common defense, M.L. and I make a united effort in the face of the worst adversity.

A small example illustrates how we work together. Every weekend we collaborate to solve the *New York Times* crossword puzzles (Saturday's and Sunday's, and sometimes Friday's too—the hardest ones of the week). We pool our mental resources rather than compete, and we've found that we complement each other's particular areas of expertise. I'm good at the short punny answers, she on the long phrases. She knows current vernacular such as "Rickroll" and texting shorthand (I don't text), plus she's incredible on scientific trivia (I didn't know "creosoted" was a word). I, on the other hand, have an embarrassing ability to draw up from the depths of memory obscure old Hollywood names and movie titles. She's an accomplished speller, while I'm a champion at finding alternative words and phrases for conveying similar ideas.

Trivial amusement, sure. But the same principles come to bear in real-life challenges. Sometimes we need these sorts of complementary skills just to get through the day! Together we're an impressive team—greater, I daresay, than the sum of our parts.

We've built our relationship—our lives—on a particular kind of interdependence. Maybe all good marriages have something similar. Do I feel guilty for needing M.L.'s help so much? No, it's more like I'm aware of it. I only apologize for it when I abuse the privilege. I think if I begged her forgiveness for circumstances beyond our control, she'd tell me to shut up. M.L. doesn't feel that apologies are necessary or appropriate for standard stuff I can't help—unless I'm unnecessarily rude.

Sometimes I curse in frustration at, say, how hard it can be to get comfortably balanced in my chair or situated pressure-free in bed. "Fuck, why can't it be better?!" I might say. After the third reiteration or so of that or some other imprecation, it behooves me to clarify that I'm cursing at the situation, not at her. She knows it, but it helps if I make the explanatory gesture. (Maybe I should heed Christina Crosby's example and find a psychotherapist I can rant to instead.)

As I've said, I make a point of not abusing M.L.'s solicitude. I try to have my paid assistants do as much as possible, which is only fair. I prefer to take care of my own needs anyway, without involving her, and she of course can use the time for herself (or, likely as not, for work or the kids). But we both know there are certain tasks only she can do right. There's no way around that.

Finally, I emerge from this exploration emboldened by an additional insight. Most couples will in time face seemingly indomitable challenges, but those of us in interabled unions may have an advantage: we've faced many of these truths sooner, not later. What we're left with are few illusions or unrealistic expectations. While I'm not going to say we're special or exceptional in any way—because when you get right down to it, we're just part of the grab bag of life—we do deal on a daily basis with what some other folks might term their worst nightmares. And we've survived. We've looked the beast in the eye and emerged undefeated. Of that, if nothing else, we can most assuredly feel proud.

ACKNOWLEDGMENTS

———◆———

THIS BOOK STARTED with an e-mail from a reader of my past work. She insisted I should write more about successful relationships. Other readers seemed to agree. You know who you are, but you might not know how much you matter.

This seed took root, nurtured by encouraging friends with whom I discussed the idea. No one was more supportive than my agent and old pal Jennifer Lyons, who has a knack for seeing potential even when others have all but given up hope. Then came Joanna Green of Beacon Press, whose intelligence, discernment, and abundant kind advocacy provided the shaping, pruning, and related necessary topiary expertise. I've now exhausted my flowery metaphor.

Needless to say, I also owe a great debt to all the people who participated in my research—some of whom are not quoted herein. And to the countless others who've inspired me (and M.L.) over the years to keep on keeping on.

INDEX

———◆———